David Strauss has an incredible background in survival and perseverance. In his newest book, *Dancing with Vampires*, you will learn that by letting go of the people and things and even thoughts that zap energy from you, you can empower yourself, build confidence and get results.

As founder of the Creative Performance Group, I created the Speakers Bootcamp, which is an intensive training that has created successful speakers, coaches, consultants, and authors worldwide. The graduates of this program are making an impact in their lives and businesses because they can speak with confidence and purpose in any situation.

David is a prime example of our elite group of graduates. He speaks and writes from the heart. The nuggets of gold you'll find in each page and with each word is truly transformational. His seven lessons will help you upgrade your thoughts and beliefs and help shape the incredible life you deserve.

Joe Williams, Strategic Expert
Specializing in Creating World-Class Speakers
www.joewilliamsonline.com

*I dedicate this book to anyone who wants to believe
in themselves and their dreams,
and has the heart and courage to overcome obstacles
and take responsibility for their own
happiness, self-confidence, and well-being.*

Dancing With Vampires

David Lloyd Strauss

Edited by

Amanda Strauss
& Barbara Wade

September 2015

Giggle Yoga, LLC
David Strauss
PO Box 28
Boulder, Colorado 80306

Ordering Information:
Quantity sales. Special discounts are available on quantity purchases by corporations, associations, and others. For details, contact the publisher at the address above.

Orders by U.S. trade bookstores and wholesalers, contact the publisher at the above address.

A Giggle Yoga Production
www.giggleyoga.com

There comes a time in your life,
when you walk away from all the drama
and people who create it.
You surround yourself with people who make you laugh.
Forget the bad and focus on the good.
Love the people who treat you right,
pray for the ones who do not.
Life is too short to be anything but happy.
Falling down is a part of life,
getting back up is living.
– José N. Harris

CONTENTS

Introduction

Have you ever had the experience of talking with someone, and when you were done you felt like the energy was sucked out of you? Or, have you ever felt like you were that person to yourself—that your own frustrations or negativity has worn you out and cast a shadow over your life? I am talking about feeling completely drained, exhausted, overwhelmed, irritated or anxious, or even stressed or depressed. If so, then you have been in the company of a Vampire.

Throughout the world, the word "Vampire" is often used as a metaphor to describe the negative people in our lives that suck the energy out of us and rob us of our happiness. It has also been used to describe our own negativity towards ourselves—our self-defeating thoughts and beliefs that drain us of our enthusiasm for life.

Using this metaphor, *Dancing With Vampires* is about helping you to become consciously aware of the Vampires in your life and how to remove their influence over you so that you can own your life, take responsibility for your own happiness, and begin to function at your highest potential—allowing you to live an emotionally rich and fulfilling life.

If you are sick and tired of being dragged down by the negative people and situations in your life, including your own negativity, then this book is for you. This is not about living a candy coated, fairy tale life where everything is perfect—far from it. Life is filled with obstacles and challenges. Rather, this is about gaining the understanding that you are responsible for the overall conditions of your life and for your own well being.

Through reading *Dancing With Vampires*, you will discover that you attract negative people and circumstances into your life and you allow them to affect you because of how you see yourself on the inside. It will become clear to you that any of your fears, failures, or feelings of inadequacy are not the result of there being something wrong with you, but rather because during your childhood development you did not learn how to properly use your mind or how to listen to your heart and intuition. Consequently, the way you think and feel and the decisions you make have been taken over by Vampires. These Vampires are mental and emotional anchors that prevent you from being your authentic self and from experiencing your true nature as an intelligent being of love and happiness. Instead of feeling and living like a creative and powerful person, you become weighted down by their grip on your life.

Just as in Hollywood, where there is always someone who has become the victim of a Vampire, in real life, many people fall victim to the Vampires of physical, mental or emotional neglect or abuse. This victimhood happens because the Vampires of neglect and abuse eat away your self-image. In turn, you continuously look outside of yourself for love and validation, you hesitate before you take action, you second-guess your confidence, and you underestimate what you are capable of. This behavior leads to you making choices that perpetuate feelings of fear and inadequacy.

When your heart and mind have fallen victim to Vampires, it is easy to forget that life is a journey of choices. Each and every day you make choices about how you see yourself, how you react or respond to life events, and where to spend your time, energy, and emotions. Each choice sets in motion its own timeline of events. Once you make a choice and take action in the direction of that choice, you cannot undo the events that unfold. Sometimes your choices will bring joy, thrills and happiness, and other times they create challenges. With every choice that you make, you can be sure of one thing—there will always be the Vampires of physical, mental, and emotional obstacles that show up along your path. Whether you let them claim control over your heart and mind or you take ownership of your life is entirely up to you.

I became fully aware of my Vampires in 2008. Shortly after the real estate and financial markets crashed, I made the choice to go on a hike to reflect upon my life, regroup, and develop a new strategy for how to move forward. That choice forever changed the direction of my life. While on my hike, exploring ancient Anasazi ruins in Chaco Canyon, New Mexico, I was hit on the head by a falling rock and faced the possibility of my own death. This unexpected turning point in my life opened my heart and mind and made me aware each moment is a decision that is based on either confidence or fear, and both of these are based on our self-image. The full story of my brush with death, and the insight that it gave me is shared in my first book, *Footsteps After The Fall.*

My journey of recovery from that "rock" experience put me face-to-face with my Vampires. It forced me to look at all the negative people in my life that were dragging me down—to face my fears, insecurities and self-doubts—and to be honest with myself about where I was in life.

At the time, I did not like what I saw, but I did not give in to my Vampires. Instead, I chose to end the game of hide-and-go-seek that I was playing with being happy. I made the commitment to do whatever it took to reclaim ownership of my life and return to being my authentic, loving self. That choice led me to the conclusion that living my life in a way that allows me to experience and express love and happiness is my highest priority.

I discovered that in order to experience your own happiness, you have to become clear about what has been blocking you from that experience. You must learn how to navigate through the people and life events that are distractions or obstacles to your happiness. You also have to forgive others that you have blamed for your pain and forgive yourself for your mistakes. Each act of forgiveness becomes a stepping stone for personal growth.

In the four years that it took for me to recover and regroup, I was deeply committed to re-discovering the secret to the type of happiness that we experienced when we were children. This discovery led me to develop an understanding of how our thoughts and emotions shape our reality. My curiosity and my unquenchable thirst for awareness led me to seven core life lessons that enabled me to let go of my past hurts and pains and redefine my self-image, my beliefs, and my principles. These lessons were transformational. They gave me the mental and emotional leverage to make a quantum leap in my self-image and in the overall quality of my life.

BOOK ONE

A ROCK AND A ZOMBIE CRAWL

*Remembering that I'll be dead soon is the most important tool I have
ever encountered to help me make the big choices in life. Because
almost everything - all external expectations, all pride, all fear of
embarrassment or failure - these things just fall away
in the face of death, leaving only what is truly important.*
– Steve Jobs

MY DANCE WITH DEATH

Life was a bloody battlefield until I conquered the enemy and won the war. Now, life is a journey, and I am a warrior. Prepared for anything and weakened by nothing. There are hills and dales, mountains and plateaus, blind spots and brilliant vistas, but none of that matters. All that matters is my second chance, and the only thing capable of disrupting my path, is myself."
- B.G. Bowers, Death and Life

It was September, 2008. I had retreated to the ancient ruins of Chaco Canyon, New Mexico to make sense of my life after the global economy had come to a screeching halt. I had lost everything and was looking for a new sense of purpose and a new meaning for my life. My answer was first disguised as a falling rock that struck my head without warning.

I started my day with inner calm and stillness in the solitude of the desert. For several hours, the vastness of the desert encapsulated my heart and mind with hope and rejuvenation. But what started out as a perfect day suddenly changed when I found myself alone in the desert, lying on the ground with my head and body covered in blood. At around 12:30 in the afternoon, I was hit on the head by a falling rock, and collapsed into that timeless moment that everyone fears—the moment of facing death. Though I do not know how long I was unconscious, when I awakened my head was spinning out of control, and I was completely disoriented. I felt the warmth of the sun on my body, yet I was shivering as if I was lying in a bathtub full of ice. My hike shifted from self-reflection and contemplation to my own self-rescue. I hiked for nearly four miles hoping that someone would find me and rescue me. It never happened. My self-rescue and the four years of recovery that followed became the incubator for my second chance at life.

The scariest moment of my entire life has since turned into the most rewarding gift I could ever receive. It took a close call with death to lead me to my life's purpose—what is now the most fun, happy, creative, and meaningful part of my life.

After my path collided with a falling rock, I had to make a decision that anyone faced with adversity has to make; do I allow myself to withdraw emotionally and become a victim of my experience, or do I look for a higher purpose and meaning and take a leap of faith to redefine who I am and what I believe? Becoming a victim would have been the easy way out because it would not have required any personal growth. I chose instead to look for a higher purpose, and it has taken an army of friends, and a lot of courage, love, gratitude, and forgiveness to help me to discover and fulfill that purpose.

I am fulfilling my new sense of purpose by sharing what I learned. I do this because I believe that we are both teachers and students for each other, and that one of the greatest gifts that we can give is to share the wisdom we gain from experience so as to challenge and empower others to learn and grow.

Whenever I share my "rock story" with others, there are two questions that are asked of me, which have inspired me to organize and share my thoughts from that experience:

1. *How big was the rock?*
2. *What are the most important lessons that you learned from this experience that you want to share with others.*

The answer to the first question is simple, and it is the most common question. I actually never saw the rock, but it was big enough to cause me to reevaluate and change every aspect of my life.

The answer to the second question took the form of seven lessons that taught me the secret to loving myself and being happy. The answers to this question formed the foundation for how I changed my life and are the basis of this book.

The Seven Lessons:

1. Surround yourself with people you can learn from

2. Self image is everything
3. Own your life
4. Your questions shape your reality
5. Life is about energy and vibes
6. Gratitude is the remedy
7. Self-love is the prize

If properly understood, these lessons can also change your life, but first you have to become aware of what it means to Dance with Vampires.

DANCING WITH VAMPIRES

An entire sea of water can't sink a ship unless it gets inside the ship.
Similarly, the negativity of the world can't put you down unless you
allow it to get inside you.
- Goi Nasu

It was serendipitous that during Halloween of 2014, a holiday that showcases fear and death, I found a way to share the lessons from my dance with death in a way that would empower others.

Every year, Denver, Colorado hosts one of the largest 'zombie' crawls in the world. Tens of thousands of people gather on the 16th Street Mall dressed up as zombies, vampires, witches, goons and countless other creatures and characters. It is one of the most animated days of the year, showing the power of imagination and creativity. It is an enormous outdoor party with people tirelessly dancing and celebrating to the extremes.

I attended the zombie crawl Halloween of 2014. As I walked down the mall covered with a white sheet in my simple ghost costume, I looked past the surface level of costumes and took a deeper look into the mindset of the crowd. It was fascinating to see the intense variety of characters and how some people went to the extremes to create very life-like images, while others were less fanatical. What is it about this holiday? Is this the one day that people feel free to completely let loose and be who they want to be and not be afraid? Do people's costumes represent a part of how they see themselves? Why is it that some people are having an outrageously fun time, while others are clearly miserable, over-intoxicated and despondent? Perhaps the zombie crawl allows people to hide in public. They can put on a costume and be outrageous without being recognized.

As I wandered through the wave of creatures, I came upon a group of Vampires who were dancing feverishly to the live jam band. I love to dance, so I went over and joined the fun. Here I was, dressed up as a ghost, dancing with Vampires. It was then that I had a moment of clarity. We dance with Vampires all the time. They are just not in costume or easily recognizable. They are the Vampires that show up every day of our life. They are disguised as the negative people who suck the life out of us and drain us of our confidence and enthusiasm; or our mental and emotional blocks and harmful habits that prevent us for doing and being our best.

When I finally walked away from the group of Vampires I reentered the sea of people in their costumes and I saw the big picture of the human experience. Life is a colorful dance of emotions and relationships. Though we will cross paths with many people during our lifetime, the most important journey we will ever have is our relationship with ourself. This relationship starts at birth and ends at death. It is a relationship between our thoughts, feelings, and beliefs and it affects our choices, actions, and results. It is a dance of courage and fear, gain and loss, youthfulness and aging. Our relationship with others is also an important part of our dance because the people we meet and share our life with shape and influence the direction of our life. For some their dance ends with death. For others, they have lived and contributed to life in such a manner that their impact becomes a self-perpetuating legacy that benefits others even after their own death.

Of all the journeys that we will embark upon, the longest distance we will ever travel is from our head to our heart. It is in that journey that we will discover what we like and do not like, who we are, and who we are not. We will also experience the full spectrum of human emotions—everything from happiness, courage, celebration and victory, to fear, sadness, abandonment and rejection.

In this time, we will also Dance with Vampires. It will not be a ballroom dance or a nightclub dance, nor will it be with the blood-sucking Vampires of Hollywood. Instead it is a dance with the Vampires that show up every day of our life. These Vampires lurk in the shadows of our heart and mind waiting for the next moment that we feel mentally or emotionally weak or vulnerable so that they can rob us of our confidence and happiness.

There are two types of Vampires hiding in the shadows: Energy Vampires and your own Inner Vampire.

Energy Vampires are the negative people who sink their teeth into your enthusiasm for life and suck the energy out of you. They are the naysayers, the Debbie Downers, and all the people who give you reasons why you are not good enough or why you will fail. They are the people who constantly complain and dump their problems on you, but do not do anything to improve their own situation. They are the egomaniacs who build themselves up at the expense of others.

Our **Inner Vampire** represents our internal conflict and turmoil, our self-defeating thoughts and beliefs, and our daily habits that undermine our happiness and drain us of our belief in ourselves and our enthusiasm for life.

Dancing with Energy Vampires and our own Inner Vampire has become such a natural part of how we think and live that we have come to accept it as being a normal and inevitable part of life. How could we not? We are constantly being bombarded with the Vampires of conflict and turmoil through the news, TV, movies, personal challenges and world events. With all the emphasis on the problems of life, it has become all too easy to forget that the world is also filled with beauty and miracles and that there are endless reasons to experience happiness and to feel grateful and fulfilled.

Living and experiencing your own genuine happiness is one of the greatest feelings in life. When you are happy everything in life seems to fall into its proper place and you feel vibrant, connected and alive. While there are a lot of people living happy, meaningful lives, many people struggle to connect with their own happiness. They may be unhappy with their career, relationships, family, friends, physical or emotional health, physical appearance, or their overall direction in life. They look in the mirror and do not like what they see. They realize that the life they are living is not the life of their dreams. They feel stuck and are looking for a way out. When this feeling of being stuck happens, most often the first thing they do is to look for a Vampire—someone or some past life event to blame—something that takes the responsibility off of themselves. They do this because it is easier to blame other people and situations for hurting them than it is to take responsibility for their own happiness and emotional choices and for the direction of their own life.

Though we are born happy and vibrant, over time life experiences pile up and weigh down on us. As we grow up, being happy becomes a choice; but life does not teach us how to make that choice. As a result, our emotions become conflicted and our Inner Vampire takes control of our life by creating masks to protect ourselves from emotional vulnerability. Each of our masks is an adaptation to fear. It can be a fear of failure or rejection, fear of loss of love, fear of being abandoned or judged, or any other fear that we can fabricate.

We create different masks for different people and different situations. Our mask may be "acting happy" when we are miserable inside. Perhaps it is telling everyone that our life is great, when deep inside we feel like everything is falling apart. It can also be falsely representing ourself as being financially successful by using credit and debt to buy things that present an image of prosperity, when in fact we are struggling. When we wear these masks, we are pretending to be someone or something that we are not. We do this because we want to be accepted by others. We would rather be a "fake somebody than a real nobody," and so we project an image of ourselves of how we want to be perceived by others because we do not know how to cope with our reality and are afraid to ask for help.

Instead of facing our Vampires head-on, we have developed the habit of dancing around them with our masks, either by pretending the Vampires are not there, or through deflecting our pain by shrinking emotionally and being a victim. We shield our heart by acting happy. We do this because it is easier to create and hide behind a mask than it is to challenge ourselves to learn and grow.

The consequence of wearing masks instead of being authentic is that we may not be aware of how deeply we have stacked our emotions until it is too late and our life begins to fall apart. These pivotal moments rarely come by choice, and they can be very uncomfortable and scary. They usually show up unexpectedly disguised as adversity—as an accident, illness, disease, loss of job, financial collapse, loss of a loved one, or the end of a relationship. But they can also show up when we have reached a pivotal moment of complete dissatisfaction with our life for any other reason. Regardless of how it presents itself, a life change will show up whether we are ready or not, and we will begin to make changes when they become a *must* instead of a *should*. The less we have paid attention to signals and signs in our own life that our life is not working, the greater the adversity. It is during our most vulnerable moments that our Vampires seem biggest and scariest.

When we reach a point of personal turmoil, it can be one of the loneliest times in our life because deep inside we know the truth—that in order for us to be happy, for things to get better, we have to transform our view of life. We have to let go of our masks and become emotionally vulnerable. We have to acknowledge our shortcomings, become open-minded and teachable, let go of the old, and make room for the new. We have to find a deeper sense of purpose and meaning and redefine who we are and what is most important to us. But, instead of facing this truth, we become stuck because our masks have become our fractured identity. We have lost touch with our true identity and our inner source of happiness. We do not know where to go, what to do, or who to reach out to in order to rescue ourselves from our own inner conflict.

At some point, each of us will come face-to-face with our Vampires. We will be presented with a life-changing experience that gives us the choice to either become an Energy Vampire—to become angry and resentful and a victim of life events—or to dig for the courage to claim power over our circumstances and take ownership of the direction of our life. With either choice, we will still be Dancing with Vampires. The difference is whether we allow them to control us, or look them confidently in the eye and tell them to get the hell out of our lives.

How To Recognize Vampires

*Before you diagnose yourself with depression, anxiety or
low self-esteem, first make sure that you are, in fact, not just
surrounded by assholes.*
- Unknown

Our Dance With Vampires in not a one-time affair. Throughout
our lives we will face many challenges that will cause us to either
shrink and withdraw or learn and grow. If we want to become a
stronger, happier person, then we have to learn how to recognize
our Vampires, and steer away from them before they emotionally
seduce us and steal our hope, enthusiasm, and energy. We have
to learn when we are being seduced by Energy Vampires or when
the negativity of our own Inner Vampire is attempting to hijack
our happiness.

ENERGY VAMPIRES
We all have Energy Vampires in our life. They are everywhere, in
all cultures, races and genders, and all walks of life. They are the
people in our lives who affect us from the outside-in. They can be
people close to us—friends, family, relatives—or people who are
a part of our daily life—neighbors, business clients, colleagues, or
even strangers.

Energy Vampires can be easily recognized. Although they do
not have fangs, you will recognize them because after you talk
with them, you will feel overwhelmed and drained of energy and
perhaps even depressed, angry, resentful, or frustrated. However
they disguise themselves, Energy Vampires are people who are
disconnected from their own inner-supply of positive emotional
energy. Just as Hollywood Vampires are on an endless pursuit

to find their next victim and suck their blood, Energy Vampires live on the energy of others so that they do not feel alone. They are perpetually looking outside of themselves for sustenance and validation—feeding off the energy and happiness of others for their own survival. They need the energy from other people just as much as they need oxygen. They are underdeveloped emotionally which they mask through coping skills that ensures that they will "get" the energy and attention that they want. They will do it at all costs, even if they need to lie. They know how to get, but not how to give.

Although there are countless negative, energy-sucking qualities that a person can have, here are five general types of Energy Vampires you will want to recognize and avoid.

Takers: Also known as narcissists, these energy suckers are all about what they can get, not what they can give. They are only emotionally available when they want something. Everything is about them. They are selfish and self-absorbed, yet can also be seductive and charming. They have strong personalities and a high need for significance and control. They have a deep need to be right and will twist their point of view to prove a point. They will provoke you with their charm and then slowly drag you into their world by making you feel "needed" by them. When they do this, it makes them feel loved, significant and in control.

Drama Queens: These are the black hole of attention cravers. They seek validation and approval at all costs. Their life is an endless soap opera of whining, disappointments, false hopes, complaints and gossip. They believe that the easiest way to get love and attention is by broadcasting their problems to everyone, until someone consoles them, gives them attention, and makes them feel validated and loved.

Blamers: These are the Debbie Downers. They live a life of blame and being a victim, never taking any responsibility for the challenges in their life. They always look for a reason outside of themselves to justify their failures and shortcomings. They live this way because they have a deep fear of rejection, and thus deflect their problems, and postpone the pain of growing and maturing.

Wannabes: They do not believe that they deserve, or can have, what they want. They always feel deprived, and rarely feel any genuine happiness for other people's achievements. They live in a continuous emotional loop of jealousy and envy. They are addicted to feeling insignificant and unworthy, so they live a life of quiet desperation. They do this because they cannot handle the uncertainty of life, and so they play small.

Crabs: These people are so negative that they claw others down to build themselves up. They are the kings and queens of insecurity and know of no other way to feel loved than to use problems as a way of getting attention. Their self-image is so low and their negativity is so powerful that they actually create problems because they know that big pain is a sure way to get love and attention.

Energy Vampires have many faces, masks and personalities. They are toxic to be around and can have a negative impact on your career and personal life when you allow them to occupy your heart and mind. If you have Energy Vampires in your life, clear them out before they sabotage your happiness and productivity, and rob you of your limited time.

INNER VAMPIRE

It is easy to recognize the people in your life that are Energy Vampires. What is much more difficult is to be honest with yourself and recognize your own Inner Vampire—your negative thoughts, beliefs and attitudes, and your self-destructive habits. Your Inner Vampire usually hides behind the veil of being a victim. It does this by deflecting problems, blaming people and past circumstances for its shortcomings.

Your Inner Vampire is best recognized by your inner dialogue— the ongoing conversation that you have with yourself in your mind. This conversation is a reflection of your self-image and continues from the moment you wake up until the time you fall asleep. It is the endless chatter of self-limiting beliefs, of making excuses, judging and criticizing yourself, and blaming others for your problems. It is a habitual form of self-sabotage. Each time you are faced with a challenge, your Inner Vampire kicks in and starts to chatter.

- What's wrong with me?
- How come I can't do anything right?
- I'll never succeed
- They will never like me
- I am just a loser

- It is not my fault
- And so on...

Most people do not have enough confidence in themselves or their abilities, and so they allow the chatter of their Inner Vampire to direct their inner dialogue and their thoughts and feelings. These inner dialogues become self-fulfilling. The more someone indulges in negative self-talk, the more they become chained to their own Inner Vampires.

We all have Energy Vampires in our lives. They show up everywhere, all the time, and feed off of our emotional weakness. The way to get rid of them is to tackle our Inner Vampire. We slay our Inner Vampire through courage and a strong commitment to personal growth.

For me, it was my deep hunger to fully embrace my second chance at life that gave me the drive and courage to tackle my Inner Vampire and disengage from the Energy Vampires that had their fangs in my life. The seven lessons that I learned became the framework for me to raise my standards and make lasting changes in every aspect of my life.

BOOK TWO

THE SEVEN LESSONS

I have learned that fear limits you and your vision. It serves as blinders to what may be just a few steps down the road for you. The journey is valuable, but believing in your talents, your abilities, and your self-worth can empower you to walk down an even brighter path. Transforming fear into freedom - how great is that?
- Soledad O'Brien

IT ALL BEGINS HERE

They say a person needs just three things to be truly happy in this world: someone to love, something to do, and something to hope for.
- Tom Bodett

During Christmas of 1981, New York City was plagued with a sanitation strike that brought trash removal to a screeching halt. By the second week of the strike, trash had piled up as high as the second floor of many buildings, and produced a nauseating stench so rancid that people had to wear masks to help them breathe. Even worse, with these excessive mounds of trash came a virtual epidemic of rats. The piles of trash were a crisis for New Yorkers, but a feast for the rats.

Imagine for a moment that you are in New York City going for a walk with a friend and they say to you, "Look at all the trash these rats brought into the city." You would look at them as if they were crazy because rats do not bring their own trash. Just as it would have been silly to blame the rats, it is just as silly to blame Energy Vampires for being the cause of your own negativity. Think of Energy Vampires as the rats of New York City. Energy Vampires only occupy your life when you have low self-image and your mind is filled with disempowering beliefs. Rats and Energy Vampires do not show up if there is nothing to eat. Energy Vampires feed off of fear and negativity because they are afraid of love. They get the best of people who are unhappy and mentally or emotionally weak. In fact, your Inner Vampire is the "trash" that attracts Energy Vampires into your life.

When you are ready to get rid of your own trash and slay your Vampires what you are really doing is acknowledging that you are not happy with your life as it is now, and you have enough dissatisfaction that you are willing to let go of what is not working and make room for new ideas and beliefs that will return you to your natural state of happiness. You are actually making a commitment to personal growth which begins with being willing to expand your view of yourself and life, regardless of how uncomfortable it may become, followed by taking clear and decisive action.

After you make the decision to commit to personal growth, it is vital to understand that your entire approach to life, including the people you associate with and all of your daily activities, is wrapped up in your identity. For example, if you have a self-defeating view of life, you will likely have attracted overbearing or controlling people into your life that enable that self-image. Once you begin to upgrade your thoughts and beliefs you are actually changing your identity. By doing this, you are putting your entire life on the chopping block, and everything is subject to change. This type of action means that you will eventually choose to let go of friendships and relationships and other parts of your life that are no longer in alignment with your new and elevated view of yourself, and replace them with people and situations which elevate you self-image and bring you happiness. This process may or may not be easy, but detoxifying your life from negativity is the natural progression from elevating your standards and moving forward.

For many people being happy seems very far away. Yet in reality, happiness is not far away. It is not a destination. Rather, it is in your own heart and mind and is discovered through a shift in your thinking. That shift is found in understanding that the secret to being happy is to detoxify your life from negative influences and begin to do things that connect you with your own happiness. You must also surround yourself with people that add to your overall well-being and who contribute to the happiness of others. If you are not doing these then change what you are doing.

Change is easier said than done. Your willingness to change and to let go of what is not working in favor of taking a new path is one of the most difficult steps to take in life. Your ability to change is dampened by your self-image. You can only do what you believe is possible. If you want to move beyond what you believe is possible, it will take a lot of courage and either a deep dissatisfaction with your life, or a significant emotional life event to give you the emotional leverage to push yourself out of the comfort of your current beliefs and into new territory of possibilities.

My significant emotional life event was when my head collided with a falling rock. But that collision was just the beginning. I was hungry for a fresh, new view of life. I did not want to backpedal and play the same old tricks in new disguise. For me, this desire for change meant one thing; I had to develop a new way of looking at myself and life. My solution was to find out how our minds work so that I could make lasting changes. I wanted to understand why we attract certain experiences and not others. Where do our Vampires come from and how do we get rid of them? How and why do we make decisions and how do we truly change our lives? I was not looking for candy-coated answers. I wanted the hard, cold facts so that I could get on track with my new life.

In order to get these questions answered, I really only had one option about what to do. I had to take massive action and start exploring new ideas and new ways of thinking that would allow me to expand my mind and elevate my view of life. This choice led me to the first of the seven lessons.

LESSON # 1:

SURROUND YOURSELF WITH PEOPLE YOU CAN LEARN FROM

The less you associate with some people, the more your life will improve. Any time you tolerate mediocrity in others, it increases your mediocrity. An important attribute in successful people is their impatience with negative thinking and negative acting people. As you grow, your associates will change. Some of your friends will not want you to go on. They will want you to stay where they are. Friends that do not help you climb will want you to crawl. Your friends will stretch your vision or choke your dream. Those that do not increase you will eventually decrease you.
-Colin Powell

Have you ever noticed that when some people fail they feel defeated while others see their failures as one more step toward success?

Prior to my dance with death I had a lot of big wins in my life. I also had a lot of failures. My wins came from my love for taking risks and making good choices. My failures came from being reckless with my choices and being overly enthusiastic, immature or inexperienced. My biggest failures came from being unteachable or following the wrong advice which led me to making choices that were lined with good intentions, but were emotionally and financially costly. In either case, I had an insatiable drive for success that was fueled by a deep need to feel loved and significant. Behind the cloak of my inner drive there were latent fears and insecurities that were steering my life without my knowledge. Vampires were in charge of my thoughts and decisions, yet I had no idea that they were present. As a result, I was not very teachable, and that is why my path collided with a falling rock and my life came to a screeching halt. Fortunately, I have since turned each of my failures into stepping stones for personal growth. They are the lessons in the classroom of life that gave me the perspective to make better choices in the future.

One of my stepping stones was learning that the only way to find answers to my questions about life was to find a mentor— someone who had the results that I wanted that I could learn from, and then follow in their footsteps. I had always known the power of having mentors, but I never understood the depth of that power until it became a critical "must" in my life.

Mentors are different than teachers. A teacher shares information. A mentor is a guide who has already achieved what you want to achieve. They have had the wins and the success and have also navigated through the pitfalls, failures, setbacks, and discouragements that are sure to be encountered along the way. A mentor has the knowledge, insights, and experience to get you results quickly and with the least amount of frustration—as long as you pay attention.

Over the years I have had a variety of mentors who have helped me to shorten my learning curve in targeted areas of my life. But now I wanted to know the fastest way to organize and improve my thinking so that I could be a sponge for new ideas and make major improvements in every area of my life. This desire for knowledge brought me to Lesson One.

Surround Yourself With People You Can Learn From

This lesson has been taught throughout history through folklore, traditions, teachers, coaches, social organizations and spiritual leaders. I was already familiar with it conceptually, but never fully grasped its power until I had a deeper sense of urgency that inspired me to do more research. After indulging my mind in volumes of reading I gained a deeper understanding of its potency. Although I was unable to identify the original source, I discovered that there is a methodical way to learn that can be broken down into four basic concepts.

1. Who do you listen to?
2. Are you teachable?
3. Thoughts vs. Actions
4. Four stages of learning

These concepts have been taught throughout the ages. When combined together they create the ideal framework for understanding the process of learning, and they solidify the importance of making good choices about the people we allow into our lives.

Together, these four concepts form a stable footing for personal growth. When you develop a daily practice of mastering these basics, you will set the stage for truly living up to your potential.

ONE – WHO DO YOU LISTEN TO?

This lesson is a game-changer for anyone who grasps the depth of its importance. Being selective about whose opinion and advice you listen to and follow is one of the most important decisions you can make. When you take advice from someone, it requires caution. There are plenty of good people with all the best intentions who can give bad advice. There are also plenty of people who are not what they say they are. Some people are masters of disguise and great at showmanship. They are either smooth talkers, or know how to project an image of success and accomplishment, though they do not have the results to match the image they project. Be wary of the "Wizard of Oz"—the big voice that seems like a knowledgeable authority, but is really only someone with a big ego hiding behind a curtain and speaking through a microphone. Make sure that the person you choose to learn from has a life that is consistent with what s/he is saying. If s/he speaks one way and acts another, then run in the other direction.

WORDS OF CAUTION: Everyone has an opinion, but not everyone has the results to legitimize their opinion. Do not ask the wrong person the right question and expect their answer to give you a solution that works. Never take advice from unproductive people. Never discuss your problems with people who are not capable of leading you to a solution. Never discuss your health problems with sickly people or your financial problems with broke people.

If you want to become physically, mentally, and emotionally healthy, you have to connect with a community of people who are doing what you want to do. You have to surround yourself with people who are already healthy and also with people who want to be healthy so that you can learn and grow with them and through them.

If you want to improve your finances, or any other area of your life, look for people who have the results you want, learn from them, and make them a part of your everyday life.

Going a step further, closely examine the people that you surround yourself with on a daily basis. The quality of your life is directly affected by the people you are consistently associated with each day. Take an honest look at your life and your friendships and relationships, and ask yourself one simple question:

Where will I be in five years if I keep doing what I am doing, and I keep spending the bulk of my time with the same type of people?

If you do not want to be in the same place in five years, then when would it be a good time to make changes?

When you are ready to move your life in a new direction, you will recognize the necessity of changing the people you are closely associated with. You do not have to "get rid" of your current friends "cold turkey." You just change your priorities of how you allot your time. When you make the choice to surround yourself with people who have the same ambitions as you, then you will see your life rapidly escalate in the direction of your dreams. You will then inadvertently and painlessly drift away from your prior network of friends, and your life will begin to blossom.

A mirror reflects a man's face, but what he is really like
is shown by the kind of friends he chooses.
- Colin Powell

TWO – ARE YOU TEACHABLE?
Surrounding yourself with people you can learn from is the first step. You also have to be teachable. If you are not teachable, then your network of people does not matter.

Being teachable is not about mental capacity, cognitive ability, or competency. It has nothing to do with genetic advantages or social or cultural advantages. Some of the greatest leaders in the world come from highly impoverished and disadvantaged backgrounds. It is all about attitude. People who are teachable have an enthusiasm for listening, learning, and applying what they learn. They have the courage and willingness to let go of old ideas habits and beliefs, and to make room in their life to learn and test new possibilities. They have a deep hunger to grow personally and to have a fuller and richer experience of life. Most importantly, they are willing to "fail" their way to success—to learn from their mistakes.

A person who is not teachable is set in their ways. They want the world to change so that they do not have to. Their ego or pride gets in the way of learning and growing. When presented with challenges, they tend to blame and act like a victim instead of using their shortcomings as a springboard and action motivator for accelerating themselves forward.

There is a difference between being taught something and learning it. Being taught means that you have been introduced to an idea. Learning something means that you have applied a concept, and found results that demonstrate that you know and understand what you have been taught. If you are not teachable, you will not learn and you will not obtain the results you want. You will only play the same old tricks in a new disguise.

How Teachable Are You?
- Do you have a high willingness to learn new ideas, accept change, and do things differently?
- Are you willing to give up something important from your day-to-day life in order to learn and grow, and self-actualize your goals and ambitions?
- How much time and money are you willing to invest to learn and practice new ideas and skills?
- Do you surround yourself with people who challenge your ideas and beliefs?
- Are you able to discuss ideas without being defensive of your opinion?
- Are you willing to let go of people and habits that hold you back from growing?
- Do you have a need to be "right," even if you are wrong?
- Are you open to other people's ideas or alternative points of view?

- Do you actively listen more than you talk?
- Are you willing to admit when you are wrong, and adopt new ideas?
- Do you like to ask questions to gain greater understanding?
- Are you willing to change your ideas and opinions based on new information?

Being teachable is one of life's greatest skills because it keeps open the door to opportunity and possibility. People who are teachable have a high willingness to learn new ideas and accept and apply change. They are willing to give up something that is an important part of their life in order to make the time and commitment to learn new ideas, test those ideas, and get results. They are willing to invest time and money in advancing their skills and awareness in areas that they want to master.

For me, becoming teachable was the most important step that I took toward ridding myself of my Vampires and taking ownership of the direction of my life.

THREE – THOUGHTS vs ACTIONS

Surrounding yourself with people you can learn from and being teachable are crucial in the path of learning. In order to make these first two steps most effective, you have to understand the relationship between thoughts and actions.

There is a common belief that what you do—your actions—are what matter most when you want to accomplish something, and that your results determine how you think and feel. This is the equivalent of saying "Ready-Fire-Aim" when shooting a firearm. If you fire before you aim, you cannot change the direction of the bullet after it is released.

When it comes to learning and getting results in your life, what matters most is your thoughts in advance of your actions. In order to get results that you want, you must put more weight on the quality of your thinking.

Thinking is all about your "why," your action motivator. It is about what's going on in your mind—your feelings, desires, dreams, goals, attitude, mental processes, objectives, intentions, motivation and emotions.

Actions are about your "how," the physical actions you take in response to your thoughts. Physical movements, strategies, techniques, actions steps, activities, plans.

Action is critical, but your thoughts have a greater impact on results than actions. Your thoughts determine your feelings and your attitude, which then determine the actions you take and the type of people and situations you attract into your life. It is easy to take action in the wrong direction in life. People do it all the time. When you become aware of how important your thinking is, you will become more strategic and intentional with your actions.

FOUR – THE 4 STAGES OF LEARNING

Learning is a life-long process. We learn from people and life events. Each person and experience that we learn from brings us unique and powerful perspectives and lessons, and prepares us for our next level of growth. No matter what we want to learn, there are four stages of learning. This sequence applies if we are a little kid wanting to learn how to ride a bike, a teenager learning how to drive, or a pilot wanting to learn how to fly. Knowing these steps makes it easier to learn because they are a simple way of measuring progress. Although I do not know the original source of these I have found them to be an instrumental part of personal growth.

Stage 1: Unconscious Incompetence

"You do not know what you do not know." This stage is pre-awareness and pre-learning. For example, when a baby is sitting in a car seat in a car, it does not know what a car is and does not even know that it is sitting in a car, or how to drive it. It is completely unaware. During this stage, an individual lacks the awareness, knowledge and skills.

Stage 2: Conscious Incompetence

"You become aware of things that you do not know." You are introduced to something new or a new idea, but you do not know what it means or how to use it. This stage is the most difficult because whether or not someone chooses to begin learning something new is determined by their self-image, and whether or not they are teachable. Using the same example, as a baby gets older, its five senses begin to develop and it becomes more aware of its environment. After many trips in the car and some physical and mental maturing, it will know that it is in a car, but does not know how to drive.

Stage 3: Conscious Competence
"You are aware of something and know how to do it." You know that you know how to do something, but you have to consciously think about it as you do it. This is the stage of learning through trial and error. Again, using the same example, the baby is now of legal driving age. It can drive, but has to think about when to brake, hit the gas and use turn signals. You are not smooth, but you can drive.

Stage 4: Unconscious Competence
"You know what you know." In this stage, you can do something without having to think about it. There may be room for improvement, but it is no longer new, and you do not have to actively think about what to do. This stage is when you are so comfortable with driving that you can sip a cup of coffee, steer with you knee and talk on the phone. I am not suggesting that you should do that, but you are self-aware enough to be able to. The challenge with this stage is that once people start getting good at something, they may stop improving. People often become comfortable with where they are and stop being teachable.

▼ ▼ ▼

When you find yourself in a situation of having to learn something new, by following these four concepts you will minimize any discomfort from learning new ideas, and maximize the speed at which you learn.

These steps taught me that it is okay to be new at something. When you move into a new direction in life, it is not always going to be smooth sailing. It takes effort and persistence to chart a new path in life. But knowing the four stages allows you to self-reflect and measure your progress, and become clear about where you need to continue to learn and grow, thus improving your self-image.

As you go through each day, pay attention to who you are listening to, remain teachable, scrutinize your thinking, and be consciously aware of which stage of learning you are experiencing. If you do this, you will thrive. If you do not, you will likely fall into your old habits of making unfavorable choices and being limited in your thinking.

LESSON # 2:

SELF IMAGE IS EVERYTHING

The 'self-image' is the key to human personality and human behavior.
Change the self image and you change the personality
and the behavior.
- Maxwell Maltz

When it comes to experiencing all that life has to offer, your self-image is everything. Most people go through life skating along with the self-image that they grew into from their childhood. They will continue to do so until they reach a turning point in their life when how they see themselves no longer works for them.

There are countless life events that can trigger the need for self-reflection and change. One of the most powerful yet difficult ways to find out who you are is to suffer great loss. It is through loss that you are given the occasion to dig deeply into your heart and mind to examine your self-image, discover your strengths and weaknesses, and to find purpose and meaning through your life events.

I discovered this truth early in my recovery when it occurred to me that my thoughts at the time of the rock fall had as much to do with my injury as gravity had to do with the rock falling—because at the time of my accident my self-image was suffering and I was ripe for change. If I had not been hit by a rock then something else would have occurred to disrupt my life. Through this insight, I developed an unstoppable sense of purpose to find someone who could teach me the power of our mind, and how to think clearly and accurately. I wanted a mentor who could demonstrate to me that what they know and teach is true based on consistent results in their own life. My quest for knowledge led me to Bob Proctor. Bob himself is a lifelong student of the greatest nineteenth- and twentieth-century teachers of the power and potential of the human mind. He learned from Napoleon Hill, Wallace D. Wattles, Earl Nightingale and Andrew Carnegie.

It was through what I learned from Bob Proctor that I began to understand that the Energy Vampires that show up in your life as well as your own Inner Vampire are mirrors of your self-image. Every person has a picture in their mind of how they see themselves. This picture is their self-image. It is either an actual picture, or it can be a set of beliefs that they hold about who they are, what they are capable of, and what they deserve.

Your picture of yourself determines how you present yourself in life. It determines your friendships, the quality of your relationships, your business and employment practices, your health, fitness, athleticism, and overall happiness. Your beliefs about yourself create your inner dialogue of the thoughts that you hold to be true and continuously repeat to yourself, either silently or out loud. By repeating them, you reinforce them, and they become a part of your core beliefs about yourself and an anchor to your identity.

Self-image is nothing more than a series of agreements that you make with yourself to believe something negative or positive about yourself. If you have a low self-image, you have made an agreement to believe that you are not worthy or not good enough due to some past event or circumstance or because someone that you love or respect has said something negative to you and you agreed to believe it.

For example, if during your childhood other kids made fun of you and told you that you are stupid, and you believed them and allowed them to hurt your feelings, then you have entered into an agreement that what other people think about you is more important than what you think about yourself; therefore, you will feel stupid. Similarly, if you think that only thin people are sexy, and someone calls you fat, you have made an agreement to believe that you are not sexy. Whereas someone else can believe that only fat people are sexy, and if someone called them fat, they would take it as a compliment. No matter what someone says to you, if it hurts your feelings, it has nothing to do with what they said, but rather that you agreed to believe what they said. Your agreement is what causes the sadness.

Your self-image creates your Inner Vampire because you can only act and feel in a way that is consistent with what you have agreed to believe about yourself. A negative self-image will perpetuate negative self-talk and self-destructive habits, because that is the natural progression of negativity. These same agreements are what attract Energy Vampires into your life, because people with low self-image agree that they do not deserve to have loving people in their life, and so they tend to attract over-bearing or abusive people who feed upon or take advantage of their weaknesses.

Likewise, if you have a healthy self-image, it is because you have agreed to believe positive, empowering things about yourself, and you will act and behave with confidence, because that is your agreement with yourself. You can change your self-image at any time by changing what you agree to believe.

Your self-image agreements are usually preceded by the words "I AM." For example, I am fat. I am ugly. I am broke. I am unloved. I am unworthy. I am a loser. Or, I am strong. I am confident. I am a winner. I am prosperous. I am loved. These agreements with yourself determine the people you associate with and the choices you make.

People with an emotionally healthy upbringing develop a strong self-image. They have the ability to overcome negativity quickly, and they rebound more easily from the challenges of life. They are aware of their Vampires, but they are emotionally self-reliant, so when their Vampires show up, they take it as a reminder that they need to redirect their thoughts and feelings to ones that are positive, uplifting and resourceful. Because of this, their Vampires have little lasting effect on their long-term happiness or well-being.

On the other hand, people who are raised with a lot of negativity develop low self-image and struggle with being consistently happy. They are quick to take things personally and easily become mentally or emotionally derailed by their Vampires. Their ability to rebound is very limited, and so they rely heavily on the validation and emotional support of others.

The foundation of your self-image is formed in approximately the first five years of your life during the initial development of your subconscious mind. It is during this time that you are most susceptible to outside influences. These influences are what cause you to be confident and self-assured or cause your Inner Vampire to take form and grow roots into your personality.

Do You Mind?

Your subconscious mind does not argue with you. It accepts what your conscious mind decrees. If you say, "I can't afford it," your subconscious mind works to make it true. Select a better thought. Decree, "I'll buy it. I accept it in my mind."
- Dr. Joseph Murphy

Isn't it odd that you can go through your entire life thinking, feeling and experiencing the world through your five senses, but never know what your mind is and how it works?

There are a lot of layers and nuances to self-image and its relationship to our mind. For me, I wanted to understand the very basics of how our mind works without going into volumes of science and research. What I learned through Bob Proctor and others completely changed my understanding of our true potential as creative and powerful beings.

Each of us has a brain and a mind. The brain is a switching station that controls and coordinates mental and physical actions of the body. The brain is a part of the body, and the body is an instrument of the mind. There are two parts to our mind: our conscious mind and our subconscious mind. Both work together with the body to shape our personality and self-image and to create our life experiences through the choices we make.

We do not have a picture of our mind because our mind is not an object. The mind is energy. It is the activity of consciousness and the energy of thought. The energy of mind is not limited to activity in our head. The mind is in everything, and everything is connected by the mind. It is in our finger, a tree, a bird, and the eye of a tiger.

In 1934 Dr. Thurman Fleet of San Antonio, Texas developed a simple diagram to visually demonstrate the relationship among the conscious and subconscious mind and the body.

The big circle represents our head and the smaller circle represents our body.

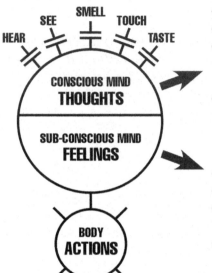

- Thinking Mind
- Can accept, reject and originate ideas
- 6 Intellectual Faculties: Will, Memory, Perception, Reason, Intuition, Imagination
- When information is impressed with repetition & emotion, it is passed on to the subconscious mind

- Emotional Mind
- Works in feelings
- Must accept all information impressed upon it through repetition or emotion
- Controls vibration of the body

We connect with the outside world and interact with our environment through our five senses of taste, touch, smell, sight and hearing, which are represented by the antennas in the above diagram. Unbeknownst to many people there are six faculties to the human mind. These faculties allow us to explore, create, and connect with our life experiences. I had been aware of these individually, but I never knew that they represent a set of tools for how to use our mind. By understanding these faculties, we can better utilize them with purpose and intention to create the experiences of our life.

The six faculties of the mind:

1. Will
2. Memory
3. Perception
4. Reason
5. Intuition
6. Imagination

Our **Will** is our ability to make choices, focus, concentrate, and commit. Willpower refers to the strength of our will. Courage, loyalty, discipline and perseverance are familiar components of will. Without will, without being "willing," we would do nothing. Our personal power is our ability to use our will to choose our thoughts, beliefs and actions, and our ability to make uninhibited decisions about the direction of our life. When we surrender our personal power to others, we are releasing our ability to think for ourselves and make our own choices.

Our **Memory** is our ability to store and recall information. We have three types of memory: short-term, long-term and sensory. Sensory memory allows us to recognize things we have already seen. All our thoughts, beliefs, and memories are stored and mapped in our brain. Every thought, belief, and memory has its own set of neuroconnections in our brain that we can draw on when thinking, reflecting, or creating. We actually have perfect memories. The problem is that we have not perfected our ability to recall our memories.

Our **Perception** is based on our beliefs, and our perception creates our reality. We actually see, feel, behave and make decisions based on what we believe. We project our beliefs, and our entire experience of life reflects back as a mirror of our thoughts and beliefs. We can only see what we subconsciously believe because the brain can only see what it is mapped to see. Our brain filters out anything that does not fit into our beliefs or that it does not think is possible. When it comes to sight and sound, we do not see and hear with our eyes and ears. We see with our mind. Our eyes and ears are instruments that collect information from the outside world and deliver it to our mind, which then interprets it based on our beliefs. When we want to change our life, we first have to change our perception. We change our perception by letting go of our idea of how things appear and what they mean to us, and open up ourselves to another point of view. When we change our perception of the moment, we actually change the moment. When we change our perception of an experience, we actually change the outcome of the experience.

Reason is the faculty of the mind that we refer to as intelligence. It is through reason that we seek to find and understand truth. Inductive and deductive logic are two forms of reasoning that we use to draw conclusions from any idea, situation, or premise.

Imagination and reason interplay as we blend ideas to formulate conclusions.

Intuition is the invisible tool of insight. Think of it in terms of the internet. Google is currently the largest search engine on the planet, storing, and exchanging remarkable amounts of information. Take all search engines together, and you would have something like a physical version of the universal mind. Not quite, though, because search engines can only store and exchange the information that we feed them. The universal mind, however, is the source and supply of all information. Intuition is a moment in time when our thoughts and feelings energetically align with a thought in the universal mind. That alignment gives us a feeling or hunch about a situation. Intuition is a form of insight... (in) sight, seeing from within.

Imagination is perhaps the most important sense—it is the basis of creativity. To imagine is to "image-within." Everything we experience through our senses and the six faculties of our mind is a reflection of imagination. Imagination is the creative use of thought. It is taking something that is not real and making it so— first in our mind, then in our reality. Imagination, with action, is what allows us to change the conditions of our life. Albert Einstein said, "Imagination is everything. It is the preview of life's coming attractions."

▼ ▼ ▼

Our conscious mind is the place where we think and reason. It is also how we connect and interact with the outside world through our five senses. It has no memory, and can only perform one function at a time. It is our awareness of the present moment— of things going on outside of us as well as mental functions happening on the inside. For example, it can be your awareness of the surroundings of where you are right now, your breathing, the temperature, the building you are in, or the chair where you sit.

Ideas of pain, sensations, perceptions, memories, fantasies, pleasure, scarcity, and abundance first originate in our conscious mind. It is through our thinking and reasoning that we have complete control over which ideas we accept and believe, or reject and discard.

Our conscious mind is a gatekeeper, a filter to our subconscious mind. Whatever ideas we accept to be true are then allowed into our subconscious mind. Anything that is allowed and accepted into our subconscious mind becomes a part of our overall system of beliefs, habits and behaviors and thus shapes all of our life experiences.

As I learned from author and mentor, Brian Tracy, our conscious mind performs four primary functions.

Identify - Compare - Analyze - Decide

As shown in the diagram with the images of the antenna, our conscious mind receives input from our environment through our six senses. It then analyzes that input in comparison to similarly stored memories in our subconscious mind, and then analyzes it. From that analysis, it decides what actions to take.

The thoughts in our conscious mind are like seeds and our subconscious mind is like the soil. We can either choose our own thoughts or we can accept them from an outside source. Whatever we allow into our conscious and subconscious minds will be expressed through our body and our senses as our experiences of life. If seeds of fear and negativity are planted, we will grow into a person who is fearful and negative. If seeds of confidence are planted, we will grow into a confident person.

Our subconscious mind is an enormous memory bank with virtually unlimited capacity. It records and retrieves everything that has ever happened to us, which it has collected through our life experiences. It consists of information that is available through memory recall that we access when we give it our focus and attention. For example, being able to walk to a familiar store without having to continuously think about where we are walking. Or, it is our ability to drive and talk on the phone at the same time because we remember how to drive without thinking about it. These types of actions help to demonstrate the fourth and final stage of learning—unconscious competence.

The subconscious mind is our "master program" for how we live our life. It is during our childhood development that our parents and authority figures influence the development of our subconscious mind. Our master program is largely written during this time.

Our master program is the sum total of all of our thoughts, beliefs and experiences. It determines what we see, and the way we think and feel. It powers our entire life experience and operates in every cell of our body. All activities and functions of the body, including all cellular activity and all automatic functions of the body such as heart rate, body temperature and breathing, are controlled through our subconscious mind. It is the place of stored memories, dreams, learned behaviors, human instincts, belief patterns, ancestral memories, and emotional patterns.

Our subconscious mind does not think or reason independently from the conscious mind. Rather, when our conscious mind gives a command, our subconscious mind obeys. Any thought that we continuously impress upon our subconscious mind becomes a part of our personality and self-image.

Our subconscious mind operates in an orderly manner and expresses itself through our feelings and actions. It will only allow us to see what it believes. Our beliefs are based upon our prior experiences which, in turn, determine our perception. Our perception impacts our decisions, which in turn affect every aspect of our life, including our health, happiness, finances, and the type of people and relationships that we attract. Since the subconscious mind only acts based on experience, it resists change and will do all that it can to keep our behavior consistent with our beliefs, prior choices, actions, and experiences.

Our subconscious mind "knows" what our comfort zone is— whatever we like and do not like—and it does everything it can to keep us in that comfort zone. Whenever we attempt to do something new or different and go outside of our comfort zone, or to change patterns of behavior, it is our subconscious mind that makes us feel uncomfortable. When we feel uneasy while trying something new, it is our subconscious mind that is trying to pull us back toward what is known, predictable, and comfortable. If we have low self-image, the subconscious mind wins, and we stay in our comfort zone. If we have a strong self-image, we more easily push ourselves outside of our comfort zone, and we actually learn and grow.

The overall "job" of the subconscious mind is to keep our daily life consistent with our self-image and our master program. This is why it typically takes deep dissatisfaction with our life or a significant emotional event to change our lives. Just as a ship will be pulled away from its place of anchor in a severe storm, the subconscious needs to be yanked away from its learned patterns and beliefs in order for it to be open to new ideas that are outside of its comfort zone.

The constant tug-of-war between our conscious desires and our subconscious habits and beliefs is what we experience as our Inner Vampire. This is the battle between our comfort zone and our true desires—between what we really want to be doing with our life, and where we actually settle. The fuel for this battle is the negative or disempowering thoughts, ideas and beliefs that were "planted" in our mind during our formative years that then grow into the mental habit of low self-image.

As we go through life collecting experiences, our subconscious mind assembles these experiences into our life story. This story is what we tell others about what happened to us. The more we believe our story, the more experiences we create and attract that are aligned with our story. If our story is of being a victim we will continue to view life through the eyes of blame, and attract more experiences to further anchor our self-image as a victim.

Our subconscious mind continuously keeps us living in the emotional residue of our past—until we do something to change our thoughts, feelings, and beliefs, thus changing our story.

What's Your Story?

If parents want to give their children a gift, the best thing they can do is to teach their children to love challenges, be intrigued by mistakes, enjoy effort, and keep on learning. That way, their children do not have to be slaves of praise. They will have a lifelong way to build and repair their own confidence.
- Carol S. Dweck

Did you know that behind every face that you see there is a story and behind every story is a person's self-image?

Each of us has a story about who we are, what has happened to us, who or what did it to us, and how it affected us. Our story is our own personal mythology. Just as religions and thought movements all over the world have mythologies that form the basis of their beliefs, each of us assembles our life experiences in our mind and creates a mythology that enables us to make sense of our life so that we can justify where we are in our life, who we are, and how we feel about ourselves. Our story has villains and heroes, victims and perpetrators, angels and Vampires. It is the story of the desire to love and be loved in return, of hopes and dreams, success and failure, happiness and sadness, fear and courage.

All of our stories have the same beginning. We start out as a seed and, through fertilization, grow into our genetic coding. Our personality and character is then shaped by our genetic predisposition and the people and environmental influences of our upbringing. Our story evolves over time and reflects our conditioning as a child and the choices we have made since childhood. Our collection of experiences between birth and death, the people we have met and the relationships that we have encountered is our story. It can be a dream come true, a recurring nightmare, or an incredible tale of personal transformation and growth.

The story we choose to tell, our myth about ourselves, depends upon the meaning we have given to our experiences. Our story can be called a myth because a myth is not always true. It is a perspective that we have created in our imagination that reflects our beliefs about ourselves and can change at any time by shifting our focus and looking at life differently.

Each of us has a powerful imagination with which we can create our reality and shape our dreams. Our imagination was most alive when we were children. We had big dreams and big aspirations. Every window and door of possibility was open to us. We had sandbox dreams. We would go to the park, play in the sandbox, and our imaginations would run wild. The sandbox was the magic place where we could imagine ourselves as anything we wanted to be. We had no limits because we had no fear. Our hearts and minds were fresh and untainted. Everything in our mind was a potential reality. We even had imaginary friends and stuffed animals that we could laugh, play, cry and hide with. As we became adults and our heart and mind became weighted down by Vampires, we began to use our imagination to magnify our fears and perpetuate our insecurities. Slowly our belief in possibilities shrank, we lost our enthusiasm and we settled for less than our full potential.

As children, at the same time that we are playing in the sandbox, we are also in the most influential part of our childhood development, the time of first impressions, which occurs during the first five years of our life. During this period we make the transition from the innocence of being a toddler to being influenced by family, friends, teachers, TV, internet, and the outside world. These influences have a substantial impact on the development of our subconscious mind.

At birth, we do not have an Inner Vampire. Our subconscious mind is a blank slate, completely open and susceptible to any and all ideas, thoughts and beliefs that are fed to us. Outside of any genetic predispositions that affect our behavior or cognition, the first impressions we receive mold us into who we are. These patterns are what determine our rules about life, love, failure, success, acceptance, rejection, confidence and fear. Our overall self-worth, our habits and behaviors, and our perception of who we are and what we are capable of, is largely determined by whether we are raised by Dream Weavers or Dream Stealers.

DREAM WEAVERS

Dream Weavers are the people who know how to have a meaningful impact on your life and make you feel good about yourself. Dream Weavers build up your self-image and make you feel loved, appreciated and significant. They understand that whatever you think and believe about yourself directly influences your experience of life. They understand self-confidence is perishable and that you have to continuously do things that reinforce and build a healthy self-image, and so they challenge you to learn and grow. As a result, they know how to talk in a way that is empowering and encouraging and builds confidence and self-love. They understand and can demonstrate the importance of being self-reliant, mentally strong, and emotionally consistent. They also understand the long-term impact of choices and actions, so they speak, behave, and lead by example in a way that builds trust and inner self-worth. They know the importance of focusing on what you are doing correctly rather than focusing on your shortcomings. Because of this, they demonstrate through their own life that failures are stepping stones to success. When you do something "wrong," they explain why it was wrong so that you can make better decisions in the future. They encourage the correct use of imagination—which is to visualize and give emotion to what you do want, not to what you do not want— and they participate in the stories you create in your mind. They teach that there is no such thing as failure as long as you are learning and growing from your actions and experiences. They demonstrate the power and importance of being focused and consistent. If you fall down, they encourage you to get up and continue. They rarely say "no" or "do not." Instead, they speak with guidance, interest and concern. Most importantly, they teach the importance of having mentors and surrounding yourself with quality people. They teach that conflict is a challenge to become stronger and smarter and that true self-worth is based on how you see yourself rather than other people's opinions of you. They treat you like a person, not like a child. And through this mutual respect, you develop a healthy self-image. Kids that are raised by Dream Weavers develop the personalities and attitudes of winners and achievers. They believe in possibilities.

DREAM STEALERS

Dream Stealers are where Vampires are created. Each of us has genetic predispositions which influence the development of our personality, but it is parenting and environment which have the biggest impact on a child's self-worth. In your first five years, your subconscious mind is a sponge. Every behavior and attitude that you see and are exposed to on a consistent basis imprints upon your mind, and shapes your personality. Toddlers do not have the ability to choose who they surround themselves with, and so they are at the mercy of their parents. This means that if they are born into a home which is abusive, or does not know how to properly raise a child, they will learn the same negative behaviors as their parents. A parent duplicates into their child their own attitude, views and beliefs. Parents who are abusive or neglectful are dealing with their own Inner Vampire, and they are duplicating that Vampire into their child. "If we hang with Vampires, we will eventually become a Vampire." This is especially true with toddlers.

Dream Stealer parents raise their children primarily through fear and anger. This can show up in many different ways. There can be physical violence, or mental or emotional abuse or neglect. It may include putting children in dangerous, unsupervised situations, or making them feel worthless by devaluing their opinion or needs. A Dream Stealer parent may vent their frustrations at their children, or give excessive punishment for even small matters. Overall, they use their children as an emotional pin cushion to relieve themselves of the pressures of life. They do not love themselves, so they emotionally jab at their children because they do not know any other way to interact, teach or discipline. Thus, children of Dream Stealers develop beliefs such as: "I am not good enough. I am a failure. I am a loser. No one will ever love me. I am stupid. I am ugly. I am fat."

Dream Stealers are not just parents. They can also be anyone who is influential in a child's life. They are the ones who tell us "you can't," warn us to "be careful" or, from a fearful place, say, "Don't do that, you may get hurt." They punish more than they encourage. Through their consistent negative input, children grow to become afraid of life. Dream Stealers put fear into your heart and mind and make you question your imagination and your creative abilities. Your natural potential as a playful, loving being becomes dwarfed by their fears, and your self-image suffers.

As children, we are in emotional conflict with our Dream Stealers. We love them out of innocence because they are people that we admire. They are most often our parents, family, teachers, religious leaders, or close friends. Because they are close to us and in positions of trust, we inherently want to believe them. But by believing them, we take on their Vampire qualities. Their fears become ours. Fear of failure. Fear of love. Fear of rejection. Fear of abandonment. Fear of scarcity. Fear of ill health. Through this imprinting, our imagination is replaced with fear, we develop self-doubt, and we start to develop beliefs about why our dreams cannot come true rather than why they can.

An upbringing by Dream Stealers is the incubator for our Inner Vampire. If the damage from the Dream Stealers is deep enough, our Inner Vampire becomes the dominant part of our personality. We then may become shy, insecure, stand-offish, resentful or withdrawn. Instead of feeling like we own our life, we can become needy and emotionally dependent on others. We then may develop beliefs that we are a victim, and adopt habits of blaming other people for our problems. If the roots of fear and self-doubt are strong enough, we may develop addictions, or any of a number of unhealthy emotional adaptations including anger, depression, isolation, rage or hostility.

These emotional behaviors and adaptations show up because we all have a need for love and connection, and a sense of certainty that we can have love in our life. If we do not know how to love ourselves or believe in ourselves, or how to feel loved in a healthy and meaningful way, we develop self-destructive patterns of behavior to compensate for these feelings of scarcity or emptiness.

As our lives progress, our predominant fears and self-doubt become the lens through which we see life. Our behavior and choices are then shaped to reflect how we see ourselves and what we believe is possible.

If we want to change our life, we have to change our story.

BE CLEAR

It is always important to know when something has reached its end.
Closing circles, shutting doors, finishing chapters, it does not matter
what we call it; what matters is to leave in the past
those moments in life that are over.
- Paulo Coelho, The Zahir

How do you change your story? Be clear.

One of the most valuable insights I gained during my recovery was learning the importance of being brutally honest with yourself about where you are in your life right now. This honesty means that you have to be clear about what the story is that you are telling yourself about who you are and how you got "here." This process is not about telling yourself the same old lies disguised as justification. Rather, it is about being honest with yourself about the overall conditions of your life. How is your health? Your finances? Your friendships and relationships? Do you see yourself as a victim, always blaming others, or are you someone who takes responsibility for your life conditions? Are you a positive, uplifting person, or is your Inner Vampire in the driver's seat of your life? Are you in a good place in your life and want to make things even better, or are you in a downswing of your life and ready to make major improvements? Either way, before you can move forward and progress, you have to be honest and clear about your story.

Up to the moment that my head collided with that rock, my Inner Vampire was in charge of my life. Although I had had a lot of amazing wins in my life, my overall self-image was very low. Like many people, I had a very turbulent childhood. As a result, my story was rooted in my past pain rather that my true potential and abilities. I was bogged down underneath emotional baggage from my youth which throttled my self-confidence and caused me to keep creating the same negative experiences in a different disguise.

Although I desperately wanted to live a better life, I was addicted to my story. Even though I was not entirely happy inside, I had told my story so many times, that I was unable to look at life differently—and for good reason. When it comes to feeling loved, we will settle for certainty, even if it brings pain, rather than taking the risk of the uncertainty of change.

The most significant part of my life story, the part that I was addicted to, started when I was thirteen. During a routine eye exam in May 1976, my mom suffered a grand mal seizure and collapsed into unconsciousness. She was immediately admitted the hospital where they discovered a tumor on her pituitary gland. After life-threatening brain surgery and radiation therapy, she was given a clean bill of health. Everyone expected her to live a full and unobstructed life. It did not work out that way. First, she began to lose her short-term memory—forgetting daily chores and activities. Then, the memory loss worsened. She was either forgetting entire segments of her life or was pulled back into the past—believing herself to be in experiences that had actually occurred ten, twenty or thirty years earlier. As her memory loss worsened, she began to experience frequent seizures. Further tests determined that the radiation therapy had damaged her brain. There was nothing to be done. Over the next two years, she suffered dozens of additional seizures. Her worst, in late 1978, threw her into coma. It ended on September 22, 1979, when she died of organ failure at the young age of 39.

Those three years of my mom's illness robbed me of my childhood. At a time when I should have been playing sports and just being a kid, I was making daily trips to the hospital. In 1978, during the time while she was in a coma, I was forced out of my home.

It was December. My sister and I had been living with our stepfather. Now we were on winter break from school, and were sent on a ski vacation to Telluride, Colorado with our father and his new wife, Cathrin. This was a fun and refreshing break from the difficulties of our daily life. But we had no idea that this trip was a pre-planned custody bait-and-switch. From Telluride, we flew to our dad's home in Seattle, fully expecting to return home to our stepfather and our life in Long Island. It never happened. With our mom terminally ill and our stepfather lacking any custody rights, the switch was made. I would stay in Seattle with Cathrin and my father, and my sister would return to New York to live with our grandparents. It would be several years before I saw her again.

I remember sitting on my father's living room couch, feeling empty and confused. I might never see my mother again, or my friends, or my East Coast family. I was lost, afraid and unsure of whom I was. Any sense of self-worth and trust I had were shattered. I had been rejected and abandoned—by those I thought had loved me.

My new life was a struggle. Not only was I starting over in an unfamiliar environment with no familiar friends, I had arrived in Seattle too far into the school year to be able to join any team sports. I was the new kid in a strange school, with a dark cloud of sadness hovering over my heart.

I survived the school year as best as I could. When the school year ended, we moved to Telluride. It was not hard to adjust to an active outdoor lifestyle, and I found it far easier to make friends in Telluride's smaller school than it had been in Seattle.

Then my mother died, and with it, all of my hope that one day she would get better and I would be able to return to the life with her that I had truly loved. The next day I was on a flight back to New York to attend her funeral. I remember being at 30,000 feet and feeling lost between my current world in Telluride, and my old world, represented by the family and friends I would soon see at the funeral.

I handled the memorial service well. But when we got to the cemetery, things were very different. In my family's tradition, immediate members of the family shovel dirt on the coffin, a symbol of burying the past and letting go. As the youngest in the family, I was to go first. Taking the shovel in hand, I dug the spaded edge of the shovel into the ground and pitched the first load of dirt onto the coffin. That was it for me. I lost all emotional composure. Burying my mother, throwing dirt on top of her coffin was the most painful experience I had ever had. To this day, that image is branded in my mind as if it happened yesterday. I may have shoveled dirt onto my mom's coffin, but I never buried her emotionally. She is still alive in my heart.

The day after the funeral, several of family members started asking about my life in Colorado. I told them that I was happy with my friends but terribly unhappy with my life. Anyhow, I said, it did not really matter where I lived anymore because my mom was dead. When a few them offered advice, I cut them short, reminding them that not one had shown any interest in my life while I was gone, so why would I listen to them now. Basically, I told them to fuck off. I would go back to Colorado and, if that did not work out, one way or another, I would find a new way to live my life.

It did not work out. First, both my grandparents died, further tearing my heart apart. Then, I just could not make Telluride work. Even though I was happy to be with my father, and I had grown to love and appreciate Cathrin as if she were my own birth mother, it was not enough. I needed and wanted more. I grasped for any type of familiarity or sense of home that I could find, but I could not find it in Colorado. What I wanted most desperately was some remnant of the life I had before my mother's death—even if it meant giving up Telluride, and returning to New York.

So, soon after, I returned to New York to live with my stepfather and his new wife. It was a disaster. My new stepmother resented me. I was the son of her husband's deceased wife, and she wanted no part of me. At night, I lay awake listening to her scream at my stepfather that he had to choose either me or her, but that he could not have both. Then I would grab my poodle, Taffy, run outside and hold him in my lap until his fur was drenched with my tears. My stepmother's disdain for me was the last straw in my emotional tolerance. I could no longer handle the deep rejection and hatred. I knew that if I did not leave, I would self-destruct. So at sixteen, I went back to Telluride on a summer vacation, and never returned to New York.

By then, my father and Cathrin had moved to Wyoming. I was living on my own in Telluride and, for the first time in a long time, there was no one around to judge me, misguide me or strangle my emotions. The day I chose to leave New York was one of the happiest of my life. Finally, I had been freed from the Vampires of my past. I would rather have been living on my own with a totally uncertain future than be in an environment of hate, wanting to take my own life.

Even though my mother was dead, I kept her alive in all my

thoughts and actions. Her love became the driving force behind my will to survive and persevere. I worked full-time in restaurants and construction while putting myself through Telluride High School and, later, the University of Colorado at Boulder. I have been moving forward ever since.

Living on my own in Telluride in the 1980s was not as difficult as I had first anticipated. The small community was very loving and supportive. Going to college at the University of Colorado at Boulder was a bit more challenging, though not because of the size of the university or the caliber of the classes, but because of the emotional challenge of feeling like an orphan with no family structure to support or encourage me. I was truly blessed by the people who had adopted me into their lives during high school, but the college environment magnified my emotional displacement. Parents' weekend and the holidays were very difficult. My commitment to working through these challenges was driven by my love for my mother and by my desire to return the favor of goodness that was extended to me. Through my passion for contribution, I sought out people, adventures and organizations that would help me to grow as a person and also give me some semblance of a family structure. I did the best I could to create my own sense of self-worth by immersing myself in the sports and fitness lifestyle and by joining social organizations that added needed structure to my life and gave me a creative outlet for social and community contribution. After I graduated from college I continued to pursue my ambition to have a meaningful impact on peoples and tested the waters of different professions that gave expression to my thirst for self-expression.

Though I found great success in all that I did, somewhere along the way I slowly began to deteriorate emotionally. This unhealthy tangent grew from deep roots of self-doubt that had been eating away at my belief in my own self-worth. I sought out answers by attending personal development seminars and broadening my understanding of basic human needs and social conditioning. Everything I learned was wonderful and contributed tremendously to my understanding of life. Yet at my core, I had not fully integrated these ideas into my life. I was happy on the outside, but sad, lonely and confused on the inside. I had no idea who I was or what I wanted, and sometimes I even questioned whether or not it was worth staying alive.

The rock hitting me on the head was the turning point for me. The physical and mental shock of impact opened my heart and revealed to me my Inner Vampire. Through the emotional peaks and valleys of that experience I grew to believe that my life could get better. This journey was not without struggle. It took me several years to regroup. But, from the day of my injury and forward, I began re-writing my story by viewing each of my life challenges as a gift which can make me a stronger and more compassionate and resilient person. Instead of seeming myself as a victim of my past, I started focusing on what I am grateful for, and how I can use my story to make a lasting difference in the lives of others.

The secret to changing your life is to change your story.

LESSON # 3:

Own Your Life

The person we believe ourselves to be
will always act in a manner consistent with our self-image.
- Brian Tracy

Has it ever occurred to you that you own your life—that your life is not something that belongs to someone else? You own it, and it is up to you to take responsibility for every aspect of the direction of your life. And if you do not, someone else will gladly step in and do it for you, and you may not like how they do it.

How do you own your life? It all comes down to clarity of heart and mind, and being honest with yourself about who you are and the current state of your life conditions. Regardless of what is going on in your life right now, if you want to step up and take ownership of your entire life, you cannot lie to yourself about anything. Any dishonesty toward yourself shatters your self-empowerment. There is power in clarity. Once you are clear and honest with yourself you unleash a dormant power that will liberate you from being manipulated by your Vampires. When you own our life, you are opening the door for transforming any difficulty into a source of inspiration and strength. You are embracing the truth that on the other side of all challenges can be found an opportunity for personal growth. This opportunity is reserved for those who exercise the courage to look beyond the current conditions and take action despite any unfavorable appearances.

When I look back upon my life, it is very clear to me that being hit on the head by a rock was no accident. I had attracted that rock to my head because the story that was then playing in my mind about my life had been ready to transform, and it had taken a blow to my head to force me into a position of being honest with myself about my thoughts and beliefs about my life.

Even though I did not die that day, at that moment when the rock hit me on the head, I truly believed that my life was ending. As a result of that experience I learned that we always have two choices. We can give in to the circumstances of life, and let them decide how we think and feel, or we can take complete ownership of our life by taking complete responsibility for our attitude, emotions, focus and choices. This means surrendering any thoughts of blame, along with any idea of being a victim.

It is easy to blame people and circumstances for your problems, and to look outwardly for reasons to justify your pain. Yet blame never helped anyone resolve anything. It certainly would not have helped me had I blamed the rock for hitting me. Blame does not fix anything. All it does is give strength to your Inner Vampire. As long as you blame, as long as you act like a victim, you are giving your power away because you cannot "fix" something if you do not take responsibility for it. Blame does nothing more than invite pain and postpone growth and denies you the ability to make changes in your life. Taking total responsibility for your life—for your thoughts, decisions and actions—is the only thing that can liberate you from your Vampires, and from the emotional bondage of low self-worth.

Our negative subconscious beliefs are our Inner Vampire. Once we are at the age where we can think for ourselves we gain the power to override our Inner Vampire and take responsibility for the experiences that show up in our life. Although we make decisions based primarily upon our subconscious habits, we are still responsible for what we think, feel, and do. No one else can make us think, feel, or act in a certain way. No one can make us feel happy or sad, ugly or attractive, loved or unloved. Ultimately, we are the ones that choose to either agree with what others say or discard their opinion. Our feelings and our choices are always a reflection of our self-image.

We may not like all the experiences that have shown up in our life. We may try to blame other people or circumstances for what has happened to us, or how we feel. But, ultimately, we are responsible for the meaning we give to each of our experiences. We always have the choice of being a Hero or a Victim.

HEROES seek solutions, accept responsibility, take action, try something new, and take control of their choices and lives.

VICTIMS are Vampires. They make excuses, blame, complain, repeat ineffective behavior and pretend problems belong to others.

Heroes ADOPT the role believing that their choices create the outcomes and experiences of their lives.

HERO

HEROES change their beliefs and behaviors to create the best results they can. They make wise decisions by consciously designing the future they want.

Seek Solutions

Accept Responsibility

Take Action

Try Something New

Take Control Of Their Choices And Lives

Make Excuses

Blame

Complain

Repeat Ineffective Behavior

Pretend Problems Belong To Others

Victims ACCEPT the role believing that external forces determine the outcomes and experiences of their lives.

VICTIM

VICTIMS keep doing what they've been doing even when it doesn't work. They make careless decisions by letting the future happen by chance rather than by choice.

No one wants to be a Victim, but many people are stuck there because of the way they think about themselves. Everyone wants to be a Hero—to feel like a winner in some area of their life. People who see themselves as Victims are obsessed with their past, but people who see themselves as Heroes learn from their past and are obsessed with their future.

When faced with challenges, those who own their life and take responsibility for their attitudes and outcomes, and exercise the courage to look within the flaws of their own character as the source of their problems, are the ones who are heroes and who grow stronger and live richer, fuller lives. They take that leap of courage because they have learned that life is an inner journey, and they understand that the people, circumstance and experiences they attract into their lives are an expression of how they see themselves.

When you claim victory over your life, you recognize that your difficulties are doorways to your greatest lessons. And your so-called "enemies," the people you dislike or fear, can be your greatest teachers in disguise.

Taking responsibility for your life is one of the greatest challenges, and offers unlimited rewards. The willingness to do so comes when someone has the courage to transform their self-image into that of being a self-empowered Hero.

Being a Hero or Victim is a choice. Unfortunately, most of us are raised to be victims, to blame people and circumstances. And it is easy to do so. Our entire culture is set up to support the blame-victim mentality. Even our legal system is based on the idea of blame-victim. Do not be like most people. Do not be a victim of circumstances or of your own neglect or ambivalence. Own your life. Believe in yourself. Take responsibility for your outcomes.

If you are not happy with the way some people treat you, then work on your confidence and become a stronger person. If you are not happy with the direction of your life, then quit observing and talking about your dissatisfaction and do something about it. If you are in a dead-end job or a tired or abusive relationship, if you are unhealthy or overweight, if you lack self-respect, or are just not satisfied, then quit wallowing in the pain. If you are afraid of love, intimacy, failure, rejection or abandonment, get over it. Quit feeling sorry for yourself and do something about it. Stop blaming people and circumstance for your sadness, your relationship problems, your emotional problems, or any of your other problems or dislikes. Stop blaming the economy for your financial problems. Stop blaming your parents or your upbringing for your problems. Stop blaming the conditions of your life on other people and outside circumstances. Get over your story of being a Victim.

You teach people how to treat you by what you allow,
what you stop, and what you reinforce.
-Tony Gaskins

Stop blaming. Own your life. Believe in yourself. Take responsibility for your own life by making the decision that regardless of what happens to you in your life, regardless of what anyone says or does to you, you are responsible for your own happiness, health, wealth and overall well-being. Cease believing that you are your past or that your past owns you. Take immediate action right now to claim ownership of your emotions and your choices and take action to demonstrate that you believe that new choice.

Get in the driver's seat of your life. Be the cause of the change in your own life. Whatever is going on in your life, you have created it by choice, neglect or ignorance. Whatever you have created, you can change. It will take courage and persistence, but you can do it. You are fully capable of taking total responsibility for your own life. It starts with the decision to do so, followed by massive action. People who take responsibility for their lives make decisions quickly, and they take immediate action in the direction of that decision.

In order to bring change into your life, you have to make room for the change. You have to let go of that which no longer serves your highest good. Let go of your old story. Let go of the people, places, circumstances and habits that are causing you to hold yourself back. Let go of unhealthy relationships and emotional entanglements that are dragging you down. Let go of people who are not loyal to you.

Some people are not loyal to you.
They are loyal to their need of you.
Once their need changes, so does their loyalty.
- Unknown

This includes letting go of disempowering and self-limiting thoughts and beliefs. Quit making excuses. Quit hiding behind your masks. Let go. Do not look back. If you want to be happy, it is your responsibility. If you want to be healthy, it is your responsibility. If you want to be financially secure, it is your responsibility. Whatever you want, it is your responsibility to shift your thinking and take new decisive action.

If you want to silence your Vampires, then quit listening to them. Instead, dig up the courage and listen to your own heart and your own intuition. Be the voice and master of your destiny. Make a decision to move forward in your new direction. Do not worry about what other people think about you or your choices. It is your life. You are responsible for your own health and your own happiness. You have to live with yourself. The only thing that matters is what you think and feel about yourself. If you do not like how you see yourself, then do something to change it.

Once and for all, release yourself from the chains and shackles of your past. Let go of your fears. Let go of your anger, grudges and resentments. Take responsibility by setting a new standard for yourself in every area of your life. Draw a line in the sand, walk away from your past and step into your dreams. Take responsibility for your attitude, thoughts, beliefs, and emotions. Take responsibility for your choices and actions. Most importantly, take responsibility for the meaning you give to each and every one of your experiences.

You and you alone get to choose what an experience means. You can change that meaning at any time. One moment something can be painful, and the next, you can see it as a blessing in disguise. If something painful happens, look for the hidden lesson, learn it, and move forward. If you cannot find one, create one. If you do not know how to create one, find someone who has the results that you want, follow in their footsteps and learn from them.

MOVE FORWARD

The only thing a person can ever really do is keep moving forward.
Take that big leap forward without hesitation, without once looking
back. Simply forget the past and forge toward the future.
- Alyson Noel, The Immortals

There is only one direction in life that is sustainable—forward. All else is an emotional trap. If you are not moving forward in your life, ask yourself this one simple question. What are you holding onto that is so important that it is worth sacrificing the rest of your life?

When you have no choice other than to transform your life and move forward, your entire game plan changes. This change means that you have to accept the fact that you cannot alter the events of your past. But you can give yourself a fresh start by changing the meaning you have given to past experiences. If you are ready for change, if you are ready to move forward, remember that you are not alone. We all have to make sense of our past, reconcile our differences, and navigate through our pains and progress. We all have to work through our choices and challenges, face our Vampires, and learn our lessons.

If you are feeling hesitant or confused about the direction of your life, or are even feeling pain from past hurts, be honest with yourself about your emotions, but do not make your pain and hurts your identity. It is okay to go through the emotions, and feel sad, empty or depressed. Just do not drop anchor and live there. You have to move on with your life. You have to move on. It is true that time heals all wounds, but you have control over how long it takes. It is different for everyone depending on their emotional maturity, but everyone chooses how long they hold onto something. The sooner you let go, the more life you get to live. How about letting go right now? Why not? What do you have to lose by liberating yourself from your past?

You are far more powerful than any challenge that life has presented to you. You do not have to go at it alone. Ask for help from someone who has the awareness and results to help you— someone who will challenge you to push yourself to learn and grow. You move forward in life by surrounding yourself with strong people, not by indulging your emotions with people who will allow you to feel sorry for yourself.

You start moving forward by first looking forward. In order to look forward, your self-image must be your priority. You must see yourself as having the same qualities as those held by people who have attained what you desire. You must do everything you can to learn and grow so that you can also become a confident, resilient person. You must see yourself as worthy and deserving of your highest good. You must love yourself and accept yourself for what you are now, and believe in what you can become.

To do so, surround yourself with inspiring and uplifting people. Seek out people who understand that victory is always first disguised as failure—that within every experience is a seed for greatness. Do not stand in judgment of what anyone has said or done to you, or what you have done to yourself. Take ownership of your life. Reclaim your power over your thoughts and beliefs. Surrender all blame. You are not your past, nor are you a victim of anyone or anything unless you choose to be. All the courage that you need to move forward is in your heart. The Hero you are looking for to rescue you is you!

When you are ready to move forward in your life, be honest with yourself. Look at your life right here and right now. Are you navigating through life by looking in the rearview mirror, or are you forging ahead with confidence and a sense of certainty and purpose? Do you have one foot in the past and the other facing forward or do you have both feet forward, facing life head-on? Are you willing to release your grip on the past for the gift of peace of mind?

You cannot create change in your life if you stubbornly blame people and circumstances for your problems. People who move forward in life know how to let go. They know how to make quick decisions and keep those decisions. They do not wait for the perfect moment to make a decision or to take action. If the circumstances they desire do not yet exist, they create the circumstances. They make things happen. If they do not know what to do, they ask for help from someone they trust who has results in their own life and can help them to move forward.

If you have mental or emotional blocks that are preventing you from making changes, they have to be released. You have to find a healthy way to let go of anger, resentment, guilt, shame, or any other negative emotion, and replace them with something positive. You have to re-purpose your pain into a new belief that empowers you.

Regardless of how you release your negative emotions, you cannot move forward if your mind is jammed with the Vampires of past pains. Negative emotions are nothing more than subconscious habits based on years of harmful programming, reinforced by years of behavior and persistent negative self-talk. The way to overcome negativity is through gratitude and forgiveness.

There are two types of forgiveness. There is forgiveness of the victim and forgiveness of the hero. Victims forgive others because they are still caught in blame, while heroes forgive themselves because they take ownership of their life experiences.

Heroes realize that regardless of what happens to them, they are responsible for the meaning they give to the experience. So, when they forgive themselves, they are simply assigning an empowering meaning to that experience. There is no blame when you own your life and accept responsibility for what happens to you.

When you finally learn to accept responsibility for your life, you step away from the emotional Vampire roller coaster and move to the highest level of self-empowerment. At this level, when you say, "I forgive you," you are really saying, "I do not blame you."

Holding on to anger, resentment and hurt only gives you tense muscles, a headache and a sore jaw from clenching your teeth. Forgiveness gives you back the laughter and the lightness in your life.
- Joan Lunden

The lesson of forgiveness teaches that we are meaning makers. The experiences of life are neutral and do not come with an embedded meaning. As your life unfolds you decide the meaning of your experiences based on your self-image and beliefs, and then you cultivate those thoughts and they become your reality. You decide whether things are "good" or "bad." You decide if you want to hold onto the past, or let go—to either learn and grow or shrivel up and die. You can grow stronger or weaker, more rigid or more flexible. You can gain more personal power or give away more power. Being forgiving does not mean that you deny or hide your emotions. It does not mean the pain or damage never existed. It simply means that you are no longer letting the pain or damage affect your life because ultimately you have the choice of whether to live in pain and have it become a part of your identity, or find greater purpose and meaning through your painful experiences.

My choice to rescue myself from being injured in the desert became an analogy for a lesson in forgiveness. All of us will have a "desert" experience. We will all have to walk through barren times in our lives where we feel empty and alone with no resources other than our own courage and faith. Those barren times usually involve something that we have been holding onto that we are struggling to release. When we choose to finally forgive and let go, we have chosen a sure path out of the desert and onward to the high road of truly being happy.

At some point in time everyone will have their own version of my falling rock, and they will be tested on their ability to move forward despite their problems. Challenges are a sign of life. If we did not have them, we would not grow. Every challenge is a response to a past decision or action. Our decisions and actions affect every aspect of our lives. We attract "rocks" because we create them. We draw into our lives the experiences that are in harmony with our thoughts, emotions, and subconscious beliefs. It does not matter what "hits" us on the head. Each and every one of us, at some point in our lives, will have a difficult experience and will have to make the choice to either take responsibility for the event and move forward or blame our "rock" for our problem. When we blame, it is because we have subconsciously developed the habit of being a victim and have given our personal power away to people, places, or circumstances.

A rock can be any painful experience. It can be childhood abuse or death of a loved one. It can be a family member, a friend, a boss, a lost lover, a teacher, a politician, the government, an injury or disease, drugs, alcohol, food or financial setbacks. It can be anyone and anything. Our rock is whatever we want it to be. It can either be the springboard that brings change into our life or the object of our blame. We can become addicted to the pain it brings or we can become empowered by the inner strength we gain. Regardless of what our rock is, we have a choice of letting it be an obstacle in our path or using it as an opportunity to forgive, learn and grow, and move forward.

My desert rock may have taken some of my blood and scalp, but through the lesson of forgiveness it gave me back my personal power and gave me the momentum to move forward. I have since made the choice that the circumstances of my life will not dictate the direction of my life. I have declared, "I am the voice and master of my destiny."

What does forgiveness offer?
Forgiveness offers everything I want.
What could you want forgiveness cannot give?
Do you want peace? Forgiveness offers it. Do you want happiness,
a quiet mind, a certainty of purpose, and a sense of worth and
beauty that transcends the world? Do you want care and safety, and
the warmth of sure protection always? Do you want a quietness that
cannot be disturbed, a gentleness that never can be hurt, a deep,
abiding comfort, and a rest so perfect it can never be upset?

All this forgiveness offers you, and more.

It sparkles on your eyes as you awake, and gives you joy with
which to meet the day. It soothes your forehead while you sleep,
and rests upon your eyelids so you see no dreams of fear and evil,
malice and attack. And when you wake again, it offers you
another day of happiness and peace.

All this forgiveness offers you, and more.

- A Course In Miracles – Lesson 122

LESSON # 4:

YOUR QUESTIONS SHAPE YOUR REALITY

The wise man does not give the right answers,
he poses the right questions.
- Claude Levi-Strauss

During the initial part of my recovery from my injury, I was caught in a negative emotional spiral. Going from hyper-athletic, mentally sharp and on the move, to short-term memory loss and being continuously fatigued was wreaking havoc on my self-image. I was definitely dancing with my Inner Vampire.

What pulled me out of my emotional struggle was when I realized the power of questions. I was first introduced to this idea by Tony Robbins, but it wasn't until this moment that I fully grasped its meaning. One evening while lying in bed, I had been stewing in my emotions and feeling sorry for myself. And then, for some reason, I realized that my inner-dialogue was a broken record of negative questions.

- How did this happen to me?
- Why can't I make my life work?
- What's wrong with me?
- Why is it so difficult to pull my life together?
- Why am I such a screw up?

My questions were based on my story. I was stuck in a loop of negative questions that were linked to my childhood. I then noticed

81

that after every question, I would feel worse. I also noticed that at other times, whenever I felt badly I was either lying down and curled up, sitting down with my body slouched over, or walking with my head down. In each of these instances, my breath would be slow and shallow and my energy low.

When we ask ourselves negative questions or are feeling sad or depressed, our posture and body language adapts to that negative emotion. Likewise, when we feel proud, happy or confident, our body language is taller and energized and our breath is deeper and stronger. I then realized that "body language" is a real thing. Our body language is a feedback mechanism that tells us the quality of our thoughts and feelings. But it works both ways; posture and body language can trigger their corresponding feelings. For example, you cannot stand tall and proud and feel depressed. And, you cannot lie down, curl up, and feel energetic and elated. This relationship means that we feel emotions and we also perform them with our physiology. Our emotions, such as sadness, depression, confidence and happiness, are closely linked to our habitual questions and our body language.

I connected the dots and saw the big picture more clearly. Our thoughts and feelings, and our ability to solve problems, are nothing more than the process of asking questions. When we ask ourselves a question, our subconscious mind immediately looks for an answer based on past stored memories. The questions we ask ourselves determine our emotional and physical response which in turn affects the quality and direction of our life. Our questions determine how we think, what we feel, what we do, how we walk and talk, and who we become. These questions can either build our self-image or turn us into Vampires.

There are empowering questions that strengthen us, or disempowering questions that weaken us. If we ask ourselves a disempowering question, "Why can't I?," we will get an answer that tells us "why we can't." Likewise, if we ask an empowering question, "How can I?," we will get a resourceful answer. The quality of the question determines the quality of the answer.

Our self-image is directly linked to the habitual questions we ask ourselves. Courage and self-confidence come from asking empowering questions: How can I? What are my resources? Who can help me? How do I need to feel in order to make this happen?

As adults, our self-image and the questions we ask ourselves are set up in our youth, based on whether we were raised by Dream Weavers or Dream Stealers.

Dream Weavers are masters of asking empowering questions. That is why they raise emotionally healthy kids. They ask questions which make kids feel like winners.

What did you accomplish today that you are proud of? This question makes them self-reflect in a way that builds self-worth.

What did you learn today? This question reinforces them to be teachable because they are receiving positive feedback for learning.

What is the funniest thing you said/saw today? This question makes them feel like being happy is very important.

What are you thankful for? This question teaches gratitude.

Did you help anyone today? This question teaches compassion.

Dream Stealers are masters of asking disempowering questions. That is why they raise kids who become Vampires. They ask questions that shrink our self-image:

What's wrong with you? When asked this question, a child will grow up thinking there is something wrong with them.

How come you can never do anything right? This question will lead a child to believe that they can never do anything right, and so they will not try, or they will self-sabotage.

How come you can't finish your homework? This question will lead a child to question his/her own intelligence. They may think that there is something wrong with them.

Why won't you listen to me? This question will cause a child to think of reasons why they do not like their parent.

As a result of being raised by Dream Stealers we are more likely to develop the subconscious habit of asking ourselves disempowering questions. Here are a few common disempowering questions that we ask ourselves.

- How come I can't lose weight?
- How come I can never finish things?

- How come I am such a failure?
- How come no one likes/loves me?
- How come people always pick on me?
- What's wrong with me?
- Why am I always last?
- Why am I always such a mess?
- Why am I not good enough?
- Why am I so fat?
- Why am I such a failure?
- Why am I such a loser?
- Why can I never do anything right.
- Why do I keep failing?
- Why do not I have any friends?
- Why is it always my fault?
- Why is money always such a struggle?
- Why is not my life working?

Each of these have the same common core belief—that there is something wrong with us, or that we are not good enough, and therefore someone else is responsible for our happiness or is the cause of our failure.

We also have something called a Primary Question, which I learned from Tony Robbins. A primary question is the one subconscious, underlying question that we ask ourselves throughout our day without even thinking about it, and it becomes the driving force for our life. A primary question can be either empowering or disempowering, depending on our self-image.

A few examples of both empowering and disempowering primary questions are:

Primary Empowering Questions
- Why am I always so lucky?
- Why is it always so easy for me to succeed?
- What do I need to do to make things better?

Primary Disempowering Questions
- What do I need to do to survive?
- How can I avoid being hurt?
- What can I do to avoid pain?

If any one of these were your underlying question each day, how do you think your life would be, and how would you feel?

Since I had moved on my own at a young age, my primary question was "What do I need to do to survive?" Thus all of my choices and actions were about surviving. Once I figured this out, I changed my question to, "what do I need to do to prosper and feel loved?" As you can imagine, my life started changing as soon as I changed my primary question.

Can you see how if you change just one question in you thinking, your entire life can change?

Dis-Empowering Question	Empowering Question
What's wrong with me?	What are my strengths?
Why can't I make my relationship work?	How can I learn to improve my relationship?
Why can't I lose weight?	How can I become healthy and fit?
Why did this happen to me?	How do I turn this setback into a victory?
How did I get stuck in this boring job?	What can I do to increase my marketable skills?
Why doesn't anyone listen to me?	How can I show other people I care?
Why do I have to work with such cranky people?	How can I show optimism to my co-workers?

The power of questions takes us directly back to the first three lessons.

One: If you are going to surround yourself with people you can learn from, you also have to know how to ask the right questions so that you can attract the right people. Being teachable means being open-minded and also knowing how to ask questions that keep you in a mindset of willingness to learn.

Two: Your self-image is your reality, because your life is the sum total of all the questions you ask yourself. A healthy self-image comes from asking empowering questions. Poor self image comes from disempowering questions.

Three: Own Your Life. Self-responsibility is the big player in the power of questions. You can only take responsibility for your life when you ask questions that build inner-strength and personal power.

It is imperative that you become consciously aware of the questions you are asking yourself. It is equally important that you learn how to recognize your disempowering questions, and reframe them into empowering questions.

When you arrive at a point in your life where you are ready, able and willing to make changes, and ready to make being happy your highest priority, change starts with asking the right questions.

Here are seven questions that will change your life.

1. Where am I in my life right now?
2. What do I really want out of life?
3. What do I need to let go of in order to get there?
4. What are my resources?
5. What do I need to do in order to get there?
6. How would it feel to actually be living my ideal life?
7. How do I make a good decision?

1– Where am I in my life right now?
You cannot set a new course for your life if you are not honest with yourself about where you are right now. For example, if you want to attract financial prosperity, but you are financially destitute right now, if you want to be healthy and fit, but are unhealthy right now, you have to be brutally honest with yourself about your starting point. This self-honestly is necessary for you

to know what type of people and resources you want to attract to move your life in a new direction.

2– What do I really want out of life?

If you were to draw a line in the sand, and one side represented where you are right now, and the other side represented where you want to be, what would that new life look like? How would you be living on a day-to-day basis that would increase your joy and happiness? This exercise is not pie-in-the-sky thinking. It is, 'what makes you happy?' If living a simple life makes you happy, then that is fine. If you want to do good for humanity, amass riches, be an athlete, fly to Mars, or re-invent the wheel, then go for it. It is okay to want whatever you want that will make you happy. Just be honest with yourself and clear in your thinking.

3– What do I need to let go of in order to get there?

Our biggest barrier to growth and progress is not the obstacles in our path, but the emotional webs that we have woven that we still hold onto but no longer serve us. None of us can move forward if we are holding onto the past. We have to let go of our Vampires and anything else that drains us of our energy and happiness. This includes people, places, memories, and things. They can be an emotionally unhealthy relationship, negative relatives or friends, an unfavorable work environment, or eating unhealthy food. It can also be watching too much news, violent or mindless TV shows, clutter in our home or office, or worn out furniture or clothing. Pretty much anything that brings our energy down.

4– What are my resources?

When you are ready to make changes in your life, when you are clear about your direction, and you have an action plan, the next step is to identify your resources. Most of the resources we will need will come from other people. Who do you know that has what you want that you can learn from? What are your financial resources? Who are your friends and family that you can truly count on to support you during your time of transition? Our greatest resource is our imagination. But even with that, we still have to be strategically resourceful and find the people, businesses and opportunities that will support our new direction. We also have to start identifying action steps that are believable to us that will propel us forward.

5– What do I need to do in order to get there?

This is a question about action. It requires being clear about where you want to go, including the emotions that will empower you, and making a written plan to get there. It is important that your plan is written so that you can measure your progress and make corrections along the way if your approach is not working. Once you do have the clarity of direction take at least one immediate action step to create momentum, and then begin to take massive action. It is critical that you take action right away so as to stamp out any initial hesitation before it turns into fear. You initial action steps can include:

- Finding a mentor
- Enrolling in continuing education classes
- Getting a new degree
- Packing up and moving
- Getting rid of things you do not need
- Buying some new clothing
- Creating a business plan

It is anything that represents taking a new and significant step forward.

6– How would it feel to actually be living my ideal life?
If you are someone who loves chocolate, or any other yummy treat, you know that your mouth can start watering just at the thought of eating it. The more we desire something, and the more real it seems to us, the faster it moves into our life. Using our imagination to get into the feeling of what our new life will be like will create a more powerful drive and sense of purpose for helping us to quickly create our new reality.

7– How do I make a good decision?
The best and most effective way to make a good, solid decision is to ask for advice from someone who has already achieved the result you want to achieve. Avoid Vampires. Never ask a broke person for financial advice or a negative person how to be happy. The only way to measure if you are getting good advice is by the results that advice has already produced for others.

Can you see the transformational power of questions? Each of them is designed to put your mind in resource mode. This means that instead of asking yourself questions that perpetuate feeling stuck, these questions cause you to take action and move forward.

How can you tell if you are asking quality questions? Pay attention to how you feel after you ask a question. People with low self-worth ask disempowering questions which make them feel badly about themselves. Confident people ask questions that make them feel empowered. Your feelings will tell you what you are thinking and what you are asking yourself.

Understanding the power of questions was transformational for me. It made me realize how one simple adjustment in thinking can change the entire trajectory of my life. It also made me realize that the questions we ask ourselves affect how other people perceive us.

Change your questions and you change your entire experience of life.

LESSON # 5:

LIFE IS ABOUT ENERGY AND VIBES

Everything is energy and that is all there is to it. Match the frequency of the reality you want and you cannot help but get that reality. It can be no other way. This is not philosophy. This is physics.
- Darryl Anka

Have you ever been around someone and thought to yourself, "they have really bad energy" or, "I do not like their vibe." Those are not just sayings. We do in fact put off energy and that energy does have a vibration that we can sense.

How is this possible? It all comes down to understanding one of the most basic scientific truths that is known and accepted worldwide. This idea is so far removed from the way we are traditionally taught to think about and view life that before I could even begin to wrap my brain around it I had to remind myself of Lesson # 1—be open minded and teachable.

We live in a universe that is made of energy, and everything in this universe is made of this same energy. Our thoughts are energy. Our feelings are energy. The sun is energy. The earth is energy. All animals and critters are energy. All things tangible and intangible are made of the same energy. Our bodies are a field of energy within a larger field of energy. The energy that lights the sun is the same energy that creates the moon. The energy that creates the clouds and the rain is the same energy that creates the thunder and lightning. The energy that creates you is the same energy that

91

creates me. All points in time and space are connected by this energy. There is no separation.

What we view as the air and space that is between us is also made of this same energy. Every entity is connected through this continuous field of energy. Everything is unique but the same. Nothing stands alone. Everything is a part of the whole. Everything is an embodiment and expression of energetic intelligence. This energy is the energy of heart and mind. There is only one self, one heart and one mind, individualized as every expression of life. This energy, this mind, in its purest form is what some call the energy of Love, Universal Intelligence, their Higher Self, or God. This love-energy is the intelligence of the entire universe. It is in everything and everything is in it. It is a magical, energetic dance of endless possibilities.

This field of energy, in all its forms, is expressed according to seven natural laws.

1. Law of Vibration
2. Law of Gender
3. Law of Transmutation
4. Law of Relativity
5. Law of Rhythm
6. Law of Polarity
7. Law of Cause and Effect

These seven laws form the boundaries which shape our reality and can be easily demonstrated through the one of nature's most precious plants—the Chinese Bamboo.

The Chinese Bamboo is one of the great teachers of life. From the moment a Chinese Bamboo seed is planted, it takes approximately five years for it to take root. In that five years there will be virtually no visible sign of vertical growth. Instead, it grows a vast network of far-reaching roots that will sustain its explosive growth and support its massive height. During that time, it will have to be watered every single day and weeds will have to be continuously pulled to ensure it is not strangled. For five years it will appear as if nothing is growing, yet it still needs to be continuously watered each and every day. After it reaches the five-year mark, it grows to an astonishing ninety feet in only six weeks. This unusual growth cycle is a perfect analogy for the seven natural laws.

THE LAW OF VIBRATION

The first law is the Law of Vibration. We know that everything is made of the same energy. Yet it is the Law of Vibration that determines the differences in the way things physically appear and behave.

Everything has its own unique frequency of vibration that is typically measured in megahertz (MHz). The way things physically appear is based on their frequency of vibration. A rose vibrates at a different frequency than a daffodil, and a rock vibrates at a different frequency than a tree. When the wind blows through a forest and howls, it creates a vibration of sound. Each string on a violin plays a different sound because each string is designed to vibrate at a different frequency. We hear music because musicians have learned to play with different frequencies of vibration.

LAW OF GENDER

Just as the Chinese Bamboo has its own cycle of growth, all else grows according to the two-fold Law of Gender.

This is the law that governs creation. It manifests in the animal kingdom as sex, and in the mineral and vegetable kingdoms as masculine-feminine energy.

This law reveals that all seeds have an incubation and gestation period. Everything in nature takes its own predetermined amount of time to move into reality; including thoughts. Each thought is a seed. Just as the Chinese Bamboo needs consistent daily watering and nurturing to grow and mature, so too must our thoughts be incubated with consistent daily feelings and actions before they can take root and move into form.

The difference between elements in nature and human thoughts is that we know the incubation period for most of nature. But the incubation period for thoughts cannot be known because each thought is unique and will have its own incubation period. What is known about human thoughts is that consistency of thought, coupled with emotion, speeds up the incubation period. Conversely, being wishy-washy, indecisive or always changing your mind interferes with the gestation period of a thought. You cannot repeatedly plant a seed and pull it out several times and expect it to take root and grow.

This law also means that it is a mistake to judge progress based on appearances. Just because you do not see visible signs of progress does not mean that nothing is germinating and taking root. Nothing is as it appears. You have to use your own judgment to determine when it is time to change your strategy or time to quit. This unknown element is why it is always best to learn from mentors, because they have already had the experience, and can tell you what signs to observe.

LAW OF TRANSMUTATION OF ENERGY

This law decrees that everything is energy and energy is in a constant state of motion and change. The non-physical is always moving into physical form. Water alone is not enough for the Chinese Bamboo to grow. It also takes nutrients from the soil, energy from the sun, combined with the daily watering and weeding to transmute the seed into a full grown Chinese Bamboo.

Whether it is the Bamboo or anything else, everything is in the process of becoming something else. The wind plants the seed. The seed geminates and is nourished by the sun, soil and water, and then grows to maturity. The seasons change. The leaves fall off the tree and become soil to provide nourishment for the tree.

All thoughts are in the process of becoming concrete things. When we think, we are creating images in our mind. When we nourish these images with consistent feelings and actions, they move through us and become the conditions and circumstances of our life. Energy is always moving through form into form and out of form.

LAW OF RELATIVITY

Does the Chinese Bamboo take five years to grow or six weeks? If you go only by what you see, it appears to take six weeks. But if you consider the years of nurturing, it takes five years. How we see things, and the meaning we give to our experiences, is relative to our thoughts, beliefs and perceptions. What is slow to one person is quick to another. What is painful to one person is liberating to another. One person's trash is another person's treasure. Everything is relative to our perception and beliefs. We see things not as they are, but as we think possible based on our own beliefs. Everything has the meaning we assign to it.

LAW OF RHYTHM

There is a rhythm to life. Everything in nature has a pulse and a beat. Things are moving to and fro, in and out. Every action has a reaction. With each rise, there is a fall. With each advance there is a retreat. The sun rises and sets. Tides go in and out. Flowers open and close. Everything in life flows harmoniously according to the Law of Rhythm. Even the Chinese Bamboo has its own rhythm that is mostly unseen during its first five years. This law is also demonstrated in how we think and feel. We will not feel good all the time. We have emotional highs and lows and physical peaks and valleys. The lows give us the contrast to enjoy and appreciate the highs. When we are in a down-swing, we still get to choose our thoughts. If we choose good thoughts we move ourself out of the valleys, and into the peaks. When we surround ourselves with quality people, we minimize our down swings and stay longer and more consistently at our peaks.

LAW OF POLARITY

Just as everything has its own flow, the Law of Polarity states that everything exists in terms of its opposite. Everything has an equal and exact opposite. Light and dark. On and off. Male and female. Up and down. If something can be good, it can also be bad. If we lose something, we also gain something. Whenever we face a challenge in life, it must also mean there is an opportunity.

This law also means that every situation is neutral. They are not good or bad until you decide if it is good or bad based on how you choose to look at the situation. If you decide that a situation is negative, you can change your perspective and look at it differently and view it as positive.

LAW OF CAUSE AND EFFECT

We reap what we sow, both in nature and in the mind. We sow with our thoughts and actions. Energy flows where our attention goes. Our beliefs determine our reality because our beliefs form our thoughts and actions and, together, create our reality. The Law of Cause and Effect is always in action. For everything we think or do, there is always a corresponding effect.

Negative energy is negative creation. Through negative thoughts and actions, you create for yourself exactly what you do not want.

These seven natural laws are always in operation whether you are aware of them or not. Life gives you everything you focus on based on the cycle of laws. There is no allowance for ignorance or misunderstanding. Each of these laws are equally important. One cannot operate without the other. For me, the Law of Vibration is the most important to understand because it is the foundation of each of the remaining laws and for addressing your Dance with Vampires. For this reason I will go into greater detail about this law.

VIBRATION AND THE
BRAIN & HEART

Thoughts are magnetic, and thoughts have a frequency. As you think thoughts, they are sent out into the Universe, and they magnetically attract all like things that are on the same frequency. Everything sent out returns to the source–you.
- Rhonda Byrne

The Law of Vibration operates through our heart and brain. Most people are unaware that there is a difference between operating from the heart or from the brain. This difference is that the minds of people who have been hijacked by Vampires function at a lower vibration and operate almost exclusively from the brain. People who operate from the brain are characterized by seeing themselves as being separate from life and tend to be more fear and victim minded. People who have been liberated from their Vampires function at a higher vibration and operate primarily from their heart, in conjunction with their brain. They see themselves as a part of a global community and tend to exhibit greater empathy, compassion and other qualities of the heart.

▼ ▼ ▼

Vibration and the Brain: On the level of thought, we are connected to this matrix of energy and vibration through our brain and our heart. Our brain is a highly sophisticated and extraordinarily powerful instrument that transforms electrical energy from one frequency of vibration to another. The information that we receive into our brain through our five senses is interpreted based on our subconscious beliefs, which shape our perception, choices, emotions and actions.

At the turn of the century, both Albert Einstein and Thomas Edison observed and proved that our brain is also a highly sophisticated and extraordinarily powerful broadcasting and receiving station designed to create and exchange different frequencies of vibration in the form of thoughts. In the same way that a smart phone can send and receive voice phone calls, text messages, photos, and even surf the internet through the air, our brain also broadcasts and receives thoughts through the air that are of the same frequency as our own thoughts.

This does not mean that we hear voices. It simply means that the brain is designed to send and receive thoughts that have a matching frequency of vibration. The brain is also a filter. There are billions of thoughts going through the air all of the time. Since every thought has its own unique frequency of vibration, your brain filters out thoughts that are not in harmony with your own thoughts or beliefs. This filter prevents you from sensory overload and keeps your life experience in harmony with your beliefs. You literally can only see what you believe. This means that in order to change what you see you must change what you believe.

The Law of Vibration has similar qualities to the Law of Attraction, but they are not the same. The Law of Vibration is actually the essence of the Law of Attraction. The Law of Attraction simply states that like vibrations are attracted to each other. This law and principle operates on all levels of life, including the level of thought.

Using the analogy of Nature the human mind grows thoughts just as a garden will grow—seeds that are planted, watered, nourished, cultivated, and harvested. If nothing is planted in a garden, then weeds will plant themselves and take over the fertile soil. All thoughts are seeds, and our consistent feelings and actions cultivate the seeds. If we do not choose which thoughts to sow, then weeds of negative thinking will take over, and Vampires will arrive.

A man's mind may be likened to a garden, which may be intelligently cultivated or allowed to run wild; but whether cultivated or neglected, it must, and will, bring forth. If no useful seeds are put into it, then an abundance of useless weed seeds will fall therein, and will continue to produce their kind.
- James Allen, As a Man Thinketh

The seeds of your thoughts are nourished with your feelings and actions. The more consistent you are with the images and feelings you hold in your mind, the quicker these thoughts will show up in your reality. Whatever you nourish, grows.

People who consistently think about, talk about, and focus on their problems, on what they are afraid of, or do not want, are actually planting, watering and nourishing the "thought seeds" of what they do not want. As a result, their life is a garden littered with experiences, the weeds, of their "don't wants." People who are afraid of going financially broke, who focus on scarcity, create the experience of living in scarcity. People who are afraid of being rejected, or fear loss of love, live in rejection. People who focus on or are afraid of illness, injury or disease, become ill or diseased. But, people who focus on happiness, health and abundance, live happy, healthy, and abundant lives.

In the same way that a gardener must continually pull the weeds from their garden, we too must pull the weeds of negative thoughts and beliefs from our mind. It takes continuous self-awareness and self-discipline to weed the negative thoughts from our mind and to harvest and cultivate positive thoughts and beliefs.

Think of the mind as an energetic loudspeaker that gives commands to the universe in the form of thoughts. These thoughts are powerful, magnetic homing beacons. When you think a thought, your brain emits magnetic particles that have the potential to attract into your life the people, circumstances and events that are in harmony with the vibration of your thoughts.

Everything that you experience is a reflection of your vibrations. Your emotions are amplifiers that tell you what you are thinking. Your emotions supercharge your thoughts, and increase the amplitude of their vibration. The higher the amplitude of vibration, the more powerful the force of attraction will be.

Positive thoughts and emotions have a high frequency of

vibration. Negative thoughts and emotions have a low frequency of vibration. We attract people and circumstances into our life that are of the same emotional vibration and frequency as our own. When you think negative thoughts, you will feel negative emotions, and will put yourself into a negative vibration, which will cause you to attract negative people and situations into your life. Likewise, when you think positive, uplifting thoughts, you will feel positive, uplifting emotions, and will put yourself into a positive vibration, which will cause you to attract positive, uplifting people and situations into your life.

The list below is an example of the energy level of some of the most common emotions. The data for this list was developed by Dr. David R. Hawkins and is found in his book, Power VS Force, which I highly recommend you add to your reading list.

Emotion	Mhz
Lower Mind-Vibration Emotions	
Shame	20
Guilt	30
Apathy	50
Grief	75
Fear	100
Desire	125
Anger	150
Pride	175
Higher Heart-Vibration Emotions	
Courage	200
Neutrality	250
Willingness	310
Acceptance	350
Reason	400

Love	500
Joy	540
Peace	600
Enlightenment	700 - 1000

As a visual example, the circular diagram below demonstrates how far one single positive or negative emotion can snowball. For example, if you feel anger, it can become aggression, resentment and jealousy.

Vibration and the Heart: Up until recently it was commonly believed that our emotions are entirely a product of the thoughts in our brain. But now there is a growing body of evidence that suggests that the heart is an intelligent organ, which has its own consciousness and "brain" and plays a much more significant role in the shaping of our emotions and our reality.

The heart is far more than the simple pump it was once believed to be. It is now recognized as a sensory organ that also receives and processes information and has its own nervous system which enables it to learn, remember, and make decisions independently of the brain. Recent research also demonstrates that the heart is in regular communication with the brain, and sends signals to the brain which influence our emotions, cognition, perception, choices, and actions.

Similarly to our brain, our heart has an electromagnetic field that communicates information throughout the body. This field changes in amplitude of vibration based on our current emotional state.

The hearts electromagnetic field has proven to be far more powerful than that of the brain. The electrical component of the heart is approximately 60 times more powerful than the brain and up to 5,000 times more powerful magnetically than the brain. The electrical component of the heart permeates and penetrates every cell in the body. The magnetic component can be detected several feet away.

We generate an electro-magnetic field of attraction or repulsion with our thoughts through the release, from our endocrine system, of hormones and chemicals known as peptides. We generate electro-magnetic charges with our thoughts that either attract to us or repel from us our experiences. Our thoughts travel through positive/negative receptors in every cell of our body and fire sequences in the neuro-net passages of our brain. These micro-electrical charges formed by our thinking are real. They influence our reality by magnetically attracting experiences of like kind to us in either a positive or negative manner, or by repelling experiences from us. Our unconscious thoughts that operate below our conscious awareness hold great power over our lives as they are firing the peptide messengers that unconsciously drive our choices.
Asara Lovejoy / Excerpt from The One Command

The combination of the thoughts in your mind and feelings in your heart is so powerful that the thoughts that you think about most consistently and supercharge with emotions are the ones that tend to show up as your reality. This does not mean that material objects will appear out of thin air. It simply means that your predominant, consistent thoughts and feelings are the most powerful force in your life. It also means that you will continue to experience your same fears and insecurities as long as you continue to give them the same emotional attention. Similarly, you will continue to thrive and feel confident as long as you give emotional charge to your positive thoughts. The universe actually bends and shapes itself to align with your habitually empowered thoughts, feelings, and beliefs.

We lie in the lap of immense intelligence, which makes us organs of its activity and receivers of its truth. The experiences of our life are a precise mirror of the music that is coming from the strings of our words, thoughts and actions. Our instrument is our heart and mind.
- Ralph Waldo Emerson

The brain-heart connection makes it clear that our reality is up to us. We are creative, thinking, feeling creatures with unlimited potential to shape the experiences of our life. We have the ability to create with our brain and heart any frequency of attraction that we want. Energies of like vibration attract each other. The more heart we put behind our thoughts, the more likely they are to become our reality.

The growing awareness of the significant role our heart plays in our life demonstrates the urgency of how important it is to pay attention to how you feel. When you fully embrace and utilize the explosive power of the heart, combined with the creative power of the brain, you become an unstoppable force in your own life.

The moment you understand that your brain and heart are continuously pulsating—transmitting and receiving thoughts and vibrations—and understand that those thoughts and vibrations shape your life experience is the pivotal moment when you can stop all blame and any thoughts of being a victim and take total responsibility for everything in your life.

Vibration and Your Body

Healing relies on an openness to the whole; a willingness to relinquish whatever frustrates or delays—mistaken ideas, negative feelings, poor diet, inadvisable lifestyle—and to accept a wider spectrum of responses with new ideas, experience, and priorities.
- Olivea Dewhurst-Maddock

Our bodies are a mass of molecules in a very high speed of vibration. They are made up of the same energy and intelligence that all thoughts and things are made of. Every cell and organ of the human body is its own reservoir of energy and has its own unique frequency of vibration within which it can exist in a healthy state. This is not a new idea. The energy emanating from the human body, often referred to as an "aura," is measurable through Kirlian photography, which was first discovered in 1939 by Semyon Kirlian. What is new is the growing awareness that we, as vibrational beings, contribute to our health and healing through our thoughts, beliefs and lifestyle choices.

Just as each thought and emotion has its own frequency of vibration, the organs of your body also have their own frequency, and so does illness and disease. Each food type also has its own frequency of vibration.

The charts on the next page give a birds-eye view of the frequency of vibration of our body, disease and common foods.

In 1992, Bruce Tainio of Tainio Technology built the first frequency monitor in the world. Through testing he made useful discoveries of the varying frequencies of the body.

Human Body Frequency:	Mhz
Average Daytime Frequency Of The Human Body	62–68
A Healthy Body	62–72
Genius Brain	80–82
Brain Frequency Range	72–90
Normal Brain Frequency	72
Human Body	62–78
Human Body - From Neck Up	72–78
Human Body - From Neck Down	60–68
Thyroid And Parathyroid Glands	62–68
Thymus Gland	65–68
Heart	67–70
Lungs	58–65
Liver	55–60
Pancreas	60–80
Illness & Disease:	**Mhz**
Colds And Flu Start At:	57–60
Disease Starts At:	58
Candida Overgrowth Starts At:	55
Receptive To Epstein Barr At:	52
Receptive To Cancer At:	42
Death Begins At:	25

Other research has measured the frequency of vibration of common food items.

Food Item	Mhz
Canned Foods	0
Chocolate Cake	1–3
Kentucky Friend Chicken	3
A Big Mac	5
Vitamin & Mineral Supplements	10–30
A Tumor	30

Raw Almonds	40–50
Fruits	65–75
Green Vegetables	70–90
Live, Fresh Wheat Grass	70–90
Your Brain	72–78
A Rose	320

Did you notice the frequency of a rose? It is off the charts. That's why people love giving and receiving roses. They give off enormous amounts of energy and raise your vibration. Now you know why you should buy yourself or your lover a bouquet of roses. It is not just a happy thought. It is the gift of high frequency vibration.

Developing the awareness that the human body, disease, and foods have their own frequency of vibration is useful in understanding the extent to which the Law of Vibration relates to your body. Your ability to think clearly and to listen to your intuition is directly linked to your overall health and wellness. Low quality, low vibration foods combined with low vibration negative thoughts are what feed your Inner Vampire. They are like tar to the flow of energy in your body and speed bumps to physical and emotional wellness.

In the same way that emotions are a feedback mechanism to show you what you are thinking, your body also gives feedback, but on a deeper level. If you have a chronic, negative or self-destructive way of thinking, if you have unhealthy eating habits, if you smoke or lack physical exercise, in many cases each of these low vibration behaviors can show up as injury or disease in the moment when your body can no longer handle the abuse. While the mind and body do have some ability to heal themselves, they too have limits. Injury and disease are a symptom of when you have reached or exceeded those limits. They are an effect rather than a cause. If you do not change your thoughts, habits, and lifestyle, the mind and body will continue to give you feedback through new or recurring injuries, or chronic pain, disease, or even anxiety or depression.

Consider this analogy. If you drove on a road covered with nails every day, would you complain about flat tires? Of course not. Flat tires are feedback that you are on a bad road. Likewise, illness, injury, and chronic negative thoughts and emotions are feedback that the focus of your thoughts is out of alignment. You change roads by changing what you are giving your energy and attention to, by improving your self-image and raising the vibration of your thoughts, feelings, and actions. Doing so allows you to attract a higher quality and less destructive life. When you become more self-aware and improve your lifestyle to be more health conscious and also raise your standards of the people you spend time with you will see your overall life improve.

When it comes to sickness, injury or disease, many people limit their approach to healing to the exclusive use of medication that deal with symptom relief but they do not adjust their lifestyle. Medications offer many benefits and they do have their place when used appropriately. When your body is displaying symptoms of sickness or disease it means your body is actually working properly. Those symptoms are feedback from your body that something is out of alignment. If you only address the symptom it does not eliminate the cause. If you continuously medicate or ignore symptoms, the dis-ease becomes chronic. Doctors can provide the wonderful service of diagnosis and offer a lot of options to guide the healing of your body. But they cannot fix your thoughts and beliefs. They cannot change your food choices or lifestyle, all of which, ultimately, have the largest impact on your overall health and wellness. Only you can do that.

You are entirely responsible for the quality of your health. Outside of any genetic predisposition for disease, if your thoughts, feelings, food choices and lifestyle habits violate the harmonic vibration of your body, sickness, injury and disease are very likely to manifest in your body. Whatever you allow into your body, heart, and mind has a direct, energetic impact on the overall health of your body, and directly affects your body's ability to heal itself. The food you eat and the water you drink either gives you energy or takes it away, depending on the quality and energetic vibration of the food and water.

You are what you consume. Your body instantly responds to everything that it is allowed to ingest. For many people, the emotional battle of their Inner Vampire—their constant mood swings and their battle with depression or anxiety can be linked to what they eat. Refined sugars and simple carbohydrates are two examples of foods that can affect your mood.

There are thousands of chemicals being added to or sprayed

on fruits, vegetables and grains. Food sprayed with herbicides, pesticides and fungicides, and processed foods filled with artificial chemicals, preservatives and sweeteners, obviously have a different impact on the body than food that is truly natural and organic. When you eat food, the closer it is to its original vibration and nutritional state in nature, the more beneficial it is to your body.

On the level of thoughts and beliefs, it is now widely accepted in western medicine that the vibration of your thoughts and beliefs has a dramatic, if not a direct impact on your physical wellbeing. In an otherwise healthy person, a chronic fear of injury or disease can actually manifest the symptom of the disease, or bring about experiences that will cause the injury. If a person is prone to injuries, it has more to do with where their minds are, what they are habitually thinking and feeling, rather than what they are doing. This is so because based on the laws of Vibration and Attraction you attract experience that match your strongest habitual thoughts.

A person's overall health is a direct match to the patterns of beliefs in their subconscious mind. The subconscious mind can only create and manifest what it believes to be true. As an extreme example, some people with multiple personality disorders will have a physical ailment or disease with one personality but not with their other personalities. Whatever manifests in the physical body has to be congruent with the reality of the subconscious mind. Based on those beliefs the subconscious mind will create health, illness, injury or disease. The subconscious mind can cause cells to become diseased, to repair damaged cells, or to "miraculously" heal instantly.

You can begin right now to feel healthy. You can begin to feel prosperous. You can begin to feel the love that's surrounding you, even if it's not there. And what will happen is the universe will correspond to the nature of your song. The universe will correspond to the nature of that inner feeling, and manifest, because that's the way you feel.
~ Rev Dr Michael Beckwith "The Secret"

Genetic defects are outside the limits to the subconscious mind. Such defects are programmed into the genes and cannot be altered. Beyond genetic defects, the environment of a human cell affects the health and healing capacity of a cell. Environment is determined by the overall vibration of your life—the quality of the air you breathe, the water you drink and bathe in, the quality of the food you eat, external social and cultural influences, and influences of the mind.

When it comes to physical healing, if you are under medical care and you want to explore or integrate the vibration-mind-body connection to healing, follow your doctor's guidance. At the same time, listen to your intuition and explore the many possibilities that a change in lifestyle can bring. There are times when the tools of western medicine are highly appropriate. There are also plenty of stories of people who have integrated western medicine with self-healing, or healed their bodies entirely through understanding the impact of thoughts, beliefs, proper nutrition and exercise. This is entirely a personal choice. Embrace whatever medical, mental, emotional and nutritional tools are available.

Our beliefs are what set the vibrational tone of our mind. Our mind is what determines what is going on in both our outside world and the inner world of the condition of our body. The healing of our Inner Vampire and of any of our ailments starts with a thought, an image in our conscious mind that then flows into our subconscious mind. The subconscious mind will accept anything that the conscious mind accepts. The images we accept control the vibration of our body, which directly affects our healing. We are totally responsible for the healing of our mind and body. It comes down to understanding the impact of our thoughts, feelings, actions and lifestyle, and to being consciously aware of what we think and feel.

Looking through the lens of my dance with the rock, when I became aware of the relationship between the Law of Vibration and physical wellbeing, I immediately became teachable and opened my heart and mind to the likelihood that I was the cause and the solution to all of my challenges.

VIBRATION AND VAMPIRES

Even though you may want to move forward in your life, you may have one foot on the brakes. In order to be free, we must learn how to let go. Release the hurt. Release the fear. Refuse to entertain your old pain. The energy it takes to hang onto the past is holding you back from a new life. What is it you would let go of today?
- Mary Manin Morrissey

Our dance with Vampires is actually a dance of vibrations. Energy Vampires are low vibration beings because they live primarily in the lower frequency emotions of fear and anger. Their low vibration is why they are continuously feeding off of other people's energy. When you attract Energy Vampires into your life it is because they are a vibrational match to your own Inner Vampire.

Our Inner Vampire is also of a low vibration because when you keep yourself living in the past, entrenched in your personal story, you fall into all the low vibration emotions that are associated with your fears and past hurts and pains. People with a low self-image will continue to live with their Inner Vampires and will continue to attract Energy Vampires because they are attracting what they are vibrating.

Whenever you feel a negative thought or emotion toward yourself, another person, or a past event in your life, you assault your mind and body with the negative vibration of that emotion, which can damage or sicken your body and which also keeps you locked in the negativity of your own Inner Vampire.

People who live in fear and anger and do not forgive will continuously attract negative experiences and Energy Vampires into their life that match the vibration of their fear and anger. As such, they will continue to experience their fears so long as they stay in the same vibration. Similarly, people who have courage and positive expectations will always find ways to win. Whatever you consistently think about and feel, you will vibrate and cause to occur.

Think of an Energy Vampire as a skunk, and their odor as their negative vibration. The spray of a skunk can be smelled as much as one mile away. Once they spray, they leave. The residue of the negative vibration from Energy Vampires lingers after they leave. If you would not want skunks lingering in your home or office, or anywhere in your life, would you want the vibration from Energy Vampires lingering in your heart and mind? If not, then you have to detox yourself from your own Inner Vampire.

Understanding the Law of Vibration makes it clear that the way to eliminate Energy Vampires from your life is to raise your vibration. The first step is to begin to heal your mind by detoxifying your life from low vibration influences and replacing them with high vibration choices.

Low Vibration Influences:
- Refrain from viewing anything that fills your mind with negativity
- Eliminate activities that waste your precious time
- Remove people from your life who take but do not give
- Let go of the past and move forward with courage
- Distance yourself from people who lie in order to get what they want
- Disengage from habits that drain your energy
- Disassociate from people who drag you down

High Vibration Choices:
- Surround yourself with people you can learn from
- Increase the quality of the food you eat and get regular exercise
- Elevate the quality of your thinking so that you build your self-image
- Improve the quality of your questions so that they are empowering
- Be teachable and have a high willingness to learn
- Find time and reasons to laugh, giggle and to be grateful
- Engage in hobbies and activities that make you feel happy and fulfilled

It all comes down to making intelligent choices, elevating self-awareness and utilizing your own personal willpower to override negativity.

When you set the conscious intention to heal your mind and overcome your Inner Vampire it is important to understand that your Inner Vampire is addicted to your low vibration negative programming. It cannot exist without it. As a result, your initial conscious intention to improve your life will be restricted by your emotional blocks and limiting beliefs. For example, if a person believes they are a victim of their family history, or of past disturbing events, they have to first work past this block before they can actually believe in the possibility of being healed of their own negativity. In addition, many people are addicted to the emotional benefits of being injured, ill or diseased which they may be reluctant to give up. These benefits can include the sympathetic love they receive and the extra assistance and attention from being physically needy. Any such limiting beliefs are walls to healing. Healing begins with abandoning any idea that you are a victim, and with deep, sincere, un-tethered belief in your healing.

There are several stages to the healing of the mind and changing patterns of thinking. First and foremost, you have to understand and accept that your thoughts and behaviors, and any chronic ways of thinking, are an out-picturing of the old, dusty beliefs that are stored in your subconscious mind. These thoughts and beliefs are like a song you cannot get out of your mind. The way to stop a repetitive song is to do the mental equivalent of scratching the CD so that it can never play again. When the scratch is deep enough, it cannot be played any more. The same is true with your thoughts and beliefs. You cannot undo or remove your thoughts, beliefs, and behavior patterns from your subconscious mind. However, you can interrupt the pattern of thinking and add new, empowering thoughts, beliefs, and ideas, which, through consistency of action and attention, will override your old thoughts and bring to form your new system of beliefs.

Thought and character are one, and as character can only manifest and discover itself through environment and circumstance, the outer conditions of a person's life will always be found to be harmoniously related to his inner state. This does not mean that a man's circumstances at any given time are an indication of his entire character, but that those circumstances are so intimately connected

with some vital thought-element within himself that, for the time
being, they are indispensable to his development.
- James Allen

At the core of raising your vibration and healing your mind is the understanding of the relationship between energy, thoughts, emotions and things. With this understanding, the next step is to pay close attention to your thoughts and to any chronic, negative, self-limiting or self-destructive thought patterns. If you are not sure of what your negative thoughts are, the best place to look is the results that have shown up in your life, including your recurring challenges, because they are a reflection of your habitual thoughts. Once you identify your negative thoughts, you can use the law of polarity to put into writing words opposite to those negative thoughts—words that are positive, empowering expressions of gratitude for the new identity and outcome. For example, fear becomes courage. "I am afraid of change" becomes "I am so happy and grateful now that I have the courage to make lasting changes in my life." Then, using your imagination with vivid accuracy and detail, you can internalize these new thoughts and create positive, happy, grateful, energizing images and feelings associated with these new thoughts. Next, you can start taking massive action by making changes in your daily routine and habits that disrupt the limiting patterns and belief, and empower and reinforce these new thoughts, feelings and images.

Detoxifying yourself from negativity and raising the vibration of your thoughts and beliefs can happen quickly or slowly. It simply depends on how much emotional leverage you have and how badly you want the change. Based on the Law of Gender, since everything has an incubation period, you must treat these new thoughts, along with the new outcome you hold for your life, with the same care as you would take with a Chinese Bamboo. You must develop a new daily habit of empowering your new beliefs through high-vibration, emotionally-charged visualization and action. Likewise, you must catch yourself in your old thought patterns as they show up. As soon as you notice that old pattern, you must immediately affirm the empowering beliefs until you develop a new, consistent system of thinking, and this new system shows up as results in your life.

Some of the most difficult work you will ever do on yourself is to examine your own thoughts and beliefs, replace them with new ones, and hold those new thoughts and beliefs consistently in your mind and reinforce them through action. The subconscious thoughts and beliefs that you have accumulated since childhood will not go away without some resistance. You overcome the resistance by tapping into your inner courage and strength. With consistency of thought and action, powered by vivid images and feelings, it can be done, and the outcome is worth the struggle.

The core principle of detoxifying your life and healing your mind is the understanding of the importance of being happy, feeling good and being grateful on a consistent basis. Claiming power over your Inner Vampire and raising the overall vibration of your life comes down to doing whatever it takes to feel positive feelings. By indulging in positive emotions and physical activity, you increase the rate of vibration of your mind and body, and positively affect your overall well being. When you emit the vibration of happiness, goodness and gratitude, when you learn to laugh and giggle at life, you unleash a whirlwind of energetic potential for positively influencing your mind and body.

PURPOSE - COURAGE - ACTION

There is one quality which one must possess to win, and that is definiteness of purpose, the knowledge of what one wants, and a burning desire to possess it.
- Napoleon Hill

If you are under the hypnosis of Vampires, is that how you really want to live, or do you want to live with excitement and positive expectations?

Life is constantly in motion. Everything changes. If you are the same person today that you were six months ago, then you are not growing. If you are not growing, then you are under the hypnosis of Vampires and likely living the same old troubles in new disguise and missing out on the full value of life.

If you are at a tipping point in your journey, remember that willingness to change comes from either profound inspiration, deep dissatisfaction with the current conditions of your life, or a significant emotional event which forces you to change. Either way, when you make that pivotal decision to move your life in a new direction, Purpose, Courage and Action are what will propel you to grow.

PURPOSE
There is power in purpose. Having purpose is having clear direction, a definite chief aim. It is being so excited about something that you do not need any external motivation from anyone or anything. You are completely teachable and willing to do whatever it takes to achieve your outcome. Your enthusiasm gets you up early and keeps you up late.

The power in purpose comes from the Law of Vibration and Attraction. When we have something definite to focus our thoughts upon that we are also consistently enthusiastic about, we activate the power of vibration and attraction. The mind always wants something to focus on. If we give it something to focus on that we are passionate about, we create a vortex of positive energy that attracts people, places and circumstances into our life that are in harmony with our purpose and help it to become a reality.

People who drift through life without purpose are like pigeons on a sidewalk. They eat the morsels that life gives them. But nothing substantial ever really shows up because they are only looking for morsels. Ideally, they want more, but they are putting out mixed signals—never focused and always changing their mind, distracted by what is directly in front of them rather than focused on what is ahead of them.

"Purpose" comes in two forms. You can have an overall life-purpose, which is what you want to focus your entire life on and also a short-term purpose, which is a goal that you want to achieve that will move you toward your life-purpose. An overall life-purpose is accomplished through achieving ongoing short-term goals.

The famous Bruce Lee had a clear and definite life-purpose statement, which he wrote down, and is now viewed online, all over the world, inspiring others through the example of his life.

"I, Bruce Lee, will be the first highest paid Oriental super star in the United States. In return I will give the most exciting performances and render the best of quality in the capacity of an actor. Starting 1970 I will achieve world fame and from then onward till the end of 1980 I will have in my possession $10,000,000. I will live the way I please and achieve inner harmony and happiness."
Bruce Lee / Jan. 1969

A short-term purpose is often referred to as a sweet-spot goal. This is something that you want to accomplish that causes you to stretch and grow toward your life-purpose. Having a sweet spot goal is very important because you can only achieve what you believe. If your big dream for life is enormous, you may not know how to accomplish it with your current level of thinking and awareness and may become easily discouraged. A sweet spot goal is a stepping stone that keeps you moving in the direction of your dream. They are mini-victories that build confidence and bring you closer to your big, juicy goal. A sweet spot goal has to be believable. If it is not, your Vampires will take over and suck the enthusiasm out of you.

If your goal is to lose 25 pounds and have a sexy beach body, but you have always been overweight, you may be enthusiastic about your goal, but you may have a lifetime of bad habits to overcome which causes low belief in your ability to accomplish your goal. A sweet spot goal may be to look at all the different ways of exercising, try a few out, and decide which one feels like the most fun and affective for you. You may try Yoga, Boot Camp, Indoor Cycling, and Cross fit, and decide that you like all of them, but you love Cross fit because you like the people that go, and the intense energy and determination of the workout. Now that you've found something that you love, you will be more inclined to do what it takes to achieve your goal, because you know that it will be both fun and challenging.

Volumes can be written about having a life purpose, how to find it, and how to go after it. For me, a life purpose is anything that puts a smile on your face, and makes you feel loved, connected and fulfilled, and makes you feel like you are contributing and growing. If working at a flower shop or ice cream parlor makes you wiggle your toes, or building a multi-national corporation gets you excited, then go for it. If you are not sure what your purpose is, then make a funny-bone list. It is a list of everything that you can do that makes you happy, and start doing them. Within that list, you will find your purpose. If you love pets, you may come up with an idea to help pets or pet owners. If you love fitness, you may come up with an idea of how to help others become more fit. If you have succeeded in accomplishing a major milestone in your life, that victory may benefit others in some way. It is generally accepted that having a life purpose that benefits others is what brings the greatest happiness and fulfillment.

For me, it was really simple. My purpose is to leverage the story of my near death experience in a way that helps others to learn and grow, and at the same time, brings joy and happiness into my life.

COURAGE
We are not born necessarily with courage, but we are born with the potential to be courageous. Courage is not an everyday emotion.

It is a reservoir of emotional strength to be drawn upon when we are ready to make a major change in our life. The change can be in any area of our life, and is usually something that will move us away from what we do not want, and toward what we do want.

Courage is like a backup battery power. It is always available when we need it, no matter what is going on in our life. It is there to help us get out of pain, or to propel us forward.

Each of us has a threshold of how much pain or uncertainty we can tolerate before we break. Courage is what helps us to make change before we reach that threshold. It is also what waits for us on the other side, if things go too far and we surpass our threshold.

Courage comes from deep within our own heart and mind. But, sometimes, when we are down, it takes someone else's belief in us, when we do not believe in ourselves, to ignite the fire of our courage. Courage does not always mean doing things ourselves. Sometimes we do need the help of others, and it takes courage to overcome our pride, and ask for that help. It is okay to ask for help. It is a sign of strength not weakness.

A courageous moment is when you look your Vampires in the eyes, when you stare into the eyes of pain, fear or struggle, and say "get out of my way" and you do not give in. When you act with courage, you have decided that taking action to get out of your comfort zone is worth the risk over the safety and security of doing nothing or remaining stagnant.

Pain, fear, and struggle will keep you in prison. Courage propels you to try new things and to look at life differently. Determination is what keeps you moving forward. However, courage and determination do not guarantee anything. You do not want to courageously head east, looking for a sunset. Instead, when you take action, you have three choices. Go at it alone, ask for advice, or find a mentor.

The first two choices are like navigating your way through a maze. Every turn in the maze is a choice. Our choices and actions determine whether we stay in the maze or find our way out. While in the maze, you may be going forward, thinking that you are moving in the correct direction, but if you make a wrong turn based on a bad choice or bad advice, you can again find yourself cornered. Fear will keep you in the corner until you muscle up the courage to start all over again.

The third choice, find a mentor, is the fastest way out. Find someone who has been through the maze and can tell you exactly what turns to make. Then you can move forward with courage and confidence.

If you can feel fear you can also feel courage. The difference between the two is that courage is having positive expectations. It is taking action with the belief that life is rigged in your favor. Fear is having negative expectations—the belief that life will not act in your favor. Those expectations are based on our self-image and on past experiences of failure or success.

A leap of courage will allow you to take new risks and accumulate new heroes that will ultimately build self-confidence. With courage, sometimes you will surprise yourself and do things you did not think you were capable of accomplishing. This success happens because what you are capable of is unlimited, and it usually takes a significant emotional event to push you past your fears and comfort zone and into a whole new level of inner strength and accomplishment. Developing a high level of courage is one of the greatest gifts you can give to yourself because it opens doors that can only be seen and experienced through a strong sense of self-worth.

Change takes courage. You have it in you. We all do! Whatever your next big step is in life, do it now. Tomorrow is never promised!

Your time is limited, so do not waste it living someone else's life. Don't be trapped by dogma - which is living with the results of other people's thinking. Don't let the noise of others' opinions drown out your own inner voice. And most important, have the courage to follow your heart and intuition.
- Steve Jobs

ACTION
Purpose and courage are paralyzed without action. Do not wait for life to happen. Infuse each moment with action. Make your own future, your own life, your own dream a reality. This is the most rewarding step in moving your life forward. It is where you get to test how teachable you are. You get to test theories, ideas, beliefs, and assumptions in the classroom of life. Nothing is truly ever learned until you take action and put ideas to the test. You will

know that you have learned when you get measureable results. If you do not get the results that you want, you simply have to change your approach and continue taking action until you do.

It is never too late for action. It is never too late to say no to your Vampires, and yes to Life. It is never too late to start over. If you were not happy with yesterday, if you did not have a sense of purpose or direction, try something different today. All changes start with action, and action starts with a decision. As soon as you decide upon a purpose or sweet spot goal, take action. Never leave the scene of a decision without taking some sort of action toward that decision.

Knowing the Law of Vibration and attraction and the power of thoughts and feelings, there is an action shortcut to getting results. It is called Future Pacing.

Future Pacing uses what some consider to be the most important of the six faculties of the mind—imagination. The power of imagination has been taught and used by astronauts, athletes, and business professionals for years, and it is highly effective. Future Pacing takes imagination to the next level. With Future Pacing, you are bringing your imagination virtually to life. You are not just visualizing in your mind, you are getting your voice, emotions and body movement fully involved in whatever you are imagining, as if it has already happened.

Future Pacing asks this simple question. How would you think, feel and act if your idea, dream or goal had just come true—literally, this moment, right now?

If you wanted to be debt free, and as of right now all your financial promises are now paid in full, how would you act and feel? You would probably feel a huge sense of relief followed by intense excitement. You would probably even jump up and down and scream with gratitude and enthusiasm: "YES, I did it!!! I am finally debt free. I am totally stoked."

Future Pacing says do not wait for your debts to be paid off in order to celebrate the victory. Celebrate right now, as if it has already happened, and then, through the Law of Vibration and Attraction, the people and circumstances will begin to line up to make it a reality. Feel your way to victory.

Your imagination is your preview of life's coming attractions.
- Albert Einstein

The most important element to Future Pacing is to literally fully involve your feelings, as if it just happened. If you have to laugh, then laugh; cry, then cry. This feeling-centric concept is not a one-time thing and then you go back to being an emotional roller coaster. It is drawing a line in time and declaring that once you begin Future Pacing, you keep yourself in the state of positive expectations, as if it has already happened, until it actually does become a reality. The trick is, do not get caught up in "how" it will happen. Your responsibility is to create the emotional state and positive expectations and let life surprise you by lining up the circumstances to make it become a reality.

This last point is crucial. One of the most common roadblocks to Future Pacing and taking action is the belief that you have to know "how" things are going to come together before you make your first move. All too often people get caught up in the "how" and they never take action. People have missed out on incredible opportunities to enrich their life because they were afraid to take the first step. There is no magical first step. There is no certainty when it comes to making decisions and moving forward. Most of what happens to you in life is off your "radar." It cannot be seen in advance. There is always uncertainty when you make the decision to move in a new direction. Everyone has a different tolerance for uncertainty. The more uncertainty a person can handle, the more possibilities can become reality. The only action you can take is to make the best decision you possibly can based on either, faith, intuition, advice of a mentor, or just the guts to try something entirely new and different.

Future Pacing is not a magic wand that can make anything happen. You also have to believe it is possible. If you use Future Pacing for something that you do not entirely believe is possible, then you will send out mixed emotional vibrations of belief and doubt which will cancel out the creative process.

Some people call Future Pacing a mental rehearsal. But you are not rehearsing. You are acting as-if it has happened. The reason this works is because the subconscious does not know the difference between imagination or reality. It is, in a very literal sense, giving your subconscious mind an audible command to listen to, and a visual map to follow so that whatever outcome you are Future Pacing becomes a reality.

You can use Future Pacing for making changes in any area of your life. It is fun and effective and life will surprise you with incredible results. It certainly has created miracles in my life. You can even use it to get rid of Vampires.

Two simple examples of Future Pacing:

"I am so happy thankful and grateful now that I own my life. I no longer let other people's negativity drag me down. I am a winner!"

"I am so happy thankful and grateful that all of my financial promises are now paid in full. It feels incredible knowing that I had the faith and courage to make this happen."

It is that simple...

LESSON # 6:

GRATITUDE IS THE REMEDY

*Gratitude unlocks the fullness of life. It turns what we have into
enough, and more. It turns denial into acceptance, chaos to order,
confusion to clarity. It can turn a meal into a feast,
a house into a home, a stranger into a friend.*
- Melody Beattie

Two years after my injury I returned to Chaco Canyon to revisit
the trail upon which I was injured. When I reached the midpoint
of the path that had soaked up my blood, sweat and tears, I took
a deep breath, sat down, buried my face in my hands, and started
crying. Two years earlier my head and body were encrusted with
blood, and I had no idea if I was to live or die. In that moment
of reflection, I discovered the single key that unlocks the door to
personal power—the key to slaying Vampires, and taking control
of every area of life. Gratitude is that key.

We know that everything is made of energy, and that everything,
including emotions, has its own unique vibration. Of all the
emotions, gratitude, along with its sister emotions, love, joy, and
bliss, has the highest vibration and is one of the greatest remedies
for curing the ails of the heart and mind. Gratitude is the eternal
elixir, the potion for all problems, the serum for success, and the
antidote for anger. It is an expression of love, and love is a gift that
can only be received when given.

There is far more to gratitude than just being thankful. Living
with gratitude is a view of life based on making decisions from the

heart. It is the Law of Cause and Effect in action. Grateful people understand that gratitude is a powerful magnet that will draw into your life that which you are grateful for. Gratitude does not judge. It does not care how much or how little you have. It only gives back in proportion to your overall feelings of gratefulness.

Gratitude is the emotional fountain of youth. It offers all a person needs. It offers peace, happiness, a quiet mind, certainty of purpose and increased self-worth. It is the valve that opens the door to hope and possibility. It is the Law of Transmutation in action. Through the power of love and forgiveness, gratitude can transmute any thought and experience into something beautiful and meaningful; but only when we choose to be grateful.

Gratitude is the sparkle in your eyes, the joy in your heart, and the happiness in your smile. When you live in a place of gratitude, you open yourself to the possibility of increase in every area of life.

Gratitude is powered by each of the seven natural laws of energy— the Laws of Cause and Effect, Gender, Transmutation, Polarity, Relativity, Vibration and Rhythm. It is the magnet that brings all these laws together in perfect harmony.

Through the Law of Vibration, we see that by consistently holding deep and intense thoughts of gratitude, we increase the amplitude of the vibration of our positive thoughts, which increases their magnetic power and speeds up the rate at which we draw the experience we desire into our life.

When we understand the Law of Polarity, we see that we do not need to make decisions based on the way situations appear at the moment, because the moment is simply a residue of the past. The Polarity allows us to look at the way things are and see them as the conditions that we want to change. It then allows us to visualize their opposite and create a new image that is focused on our desired direction and outcome. Gratitude is the vacuum that pulls us out of that residue and draws all new possibilities into our life. It is the gateway that opens the flow of miracles.

When we lack gratitude, we lack everything. Just as gratitude draws all possibilities into our life, a lack of gratitude creates the resistance that prevents the flow of abundance. If we experience scarcity in any area of our life, it is because we lack gratitude in that area. For example, the Law of Cause and Effect makes it very clear—in order for any result (effect) to take form, it must first have a cause. It must be initiated with a clear image in our mind and consistent thoughts and feelings. We have to believe it to be real before it has actually become real. Gratitude is a cause, not an effect. Feeling grateful is what attracts goodness into our lives. When we feel grateful for what we desire with the same intensity as if we already had it, we unleash energetic forces that will flood our life with miracles.

Gratitude takes emotional maturity. While most people allow their problems to bring them down, people who are grateful understand that behind every challenge is an opportunity to learn and grow. By living in gratitude, we choose to see this moment as what we want it to be, regardless of what has happened or appears to be happening. We see it as fertile soil to plant new seeds of thought.

All our personal power is found in this moment in time, not in the past or future. How we think and feel during this moment in time is what creates the energy that defines the next moment and activates what will manifest in our life down the road. Thoughts of gratitude should be our first thoughts in the morning and the lullaby that we sing to ourselves at night.

To be grateful is to be truly obedient to the Law of Gender. We cannot have faith and doubt at the same time. Gratitude loves consistency. Everything takes time. To allow gratitude to fully bless our life, we have to allow our dreams and desires to align in their own time.

When we are ready to make a change in the direction of our life, the fastest way to initiate that change is to enter into a place of deep emotional gratitude. We do this by focusing on everything we have in or life right now, that we can be grateful for, and to carry that feeling of gratitude toward the things we want, as if we already had them.

Gratitude is the remedy to rid your life of Vampires. Just as Hollywood Vampires are killed by light, so too are Energy Vampires and our Inner Vampire killed by the light of Gratitude.

Mastering Gratitude is the key to being happy.

LESSON # 7:

SELF LOVE IS THE PRIZE

You've got it all wrong. You did not come here to master unconditional love. That is where you came from and where you'll return. You came here to learn personal love. Universal love. Messy love. Sweaty love. Crazy love. Broken love. Whole love. Infused with divinity. Lived through the grace of stumbling. Demonstrated through the beauty of... messing up—often. You did not come here to be perfect. You already are. You came here to be gorgeously human. Flawed and fabulous. And then to rise again into remembering.
- Unknown

The first six lessons are valuable tools and insights for helping you to take ownership of your life and responsibility for your own happiness. Together, they serve the purpose of giving you a way to self-reflect, and provide you with new choices for adding clarity and structure to the way you see yourself and live your life.

The seventh and final lesson—the lesson of self-love—presents one of life's greatest challenges because there is no handbook for self-love, nor is it a destination where you arrive to find that you suddenly love and accept who you are, and life is a bed of roses. Rather, it is a shift in perspective, a point of mental clarity and emotional peace and maturity that allows you to accept challenges as a necessary and beneficial part of personal growth. It is when you no longer take life personally and can flow with life's changes without being consumed by the fluctuations. Ultimately, it comes down to accepting yourself as you are and knowing how to live your life in a way that gives expression to your inner happiness while not concerning yourself with other people's opinions of you.

The road to that place of inner clarity and peace is not smooth. There are countless obstacles, challenges and distractions which push against your identity and your ability to expand your understanding of who you are and what it means to love yourself. This resistance is a natural part of life and does not go away. It will follow you through every stage of life, and keep you forever looking outside of yourself for the secret to loving yourself and being happy—until you reach a moment of complete dissatisfaction with your life as it is or are forced to change by a significant emotional event.

From the moment you are born to the second you die, your obstacles, challenges, and distractions will put your identity into in a constant state of flux and transformation. Every new experience will cause you to look at yourself and life differently. During your lifetime, how you see yourself—your self-identity—will transition through two major stages of change and possibly a third.

The first stage is the self you are born with. It is when your subconscious mind is a blank slate with no personality, no life experience and no memories. This state is your authentic self— the real you that is one with all of life without the layers of fear and pain and without masks or Vampires. In this stage happiness is your natural state because it reflects the truth that you are love.

The second stage is the self you are raised to be. This is your personality and character that has been shaped by your environment and upbringing. This is the self that is ruled by your thoughts and beliefs and the habits of your subconscious mind. Through this perspective, you see yourself as being separate from others, and life is something that happens to you, rather than your experiences being a reflection of your thoughts and beliefs. This is the self that most people do not like or love and is also the self in which the majority of people will live and die. It is the self that either lives with fear and identifies with the pains of the past and is under the hypnosis of Vampires—or is confident but has not yet developed its own identity outside of the influences and expectations of your upbringing.

Finally, there is the return to your authentic self which begins to take shape the moment you stop identifying with the fears and challenges that your personality and character have accumulated and start taking full responsibility for your entire life. This stage is the rebirth of your true nature as a being of love, joy, and happiness, empowered with the wisdom that comes from experience and the courage that comes with the passage of time. This is the self that has danced with Vampires and has broken free from their grip on your heart and mind. This is the self that had the courage to ask empowering questions and embraced the power of forgiveness and gratitude. This is the you that you love and have always wanted to return to being. It is your true identity as a confident, self-assured, creative being living with a sense of purpose and enthusiasm for life.

Moving from the second to third stage of self-identity is the journey to self-love. Only a small number of people will ever embark upon the re-discovery of this self. For those who do, the rewards are immeasurable.

In order to become clear about what self-love is, it is important to first be clear about what it is not. Everyone has different ideas and rules about what it means to be loved. Since there is no handbook for self-love, and to feel loved is a basic human need, people will naturally default to looking outside of themselves for love, connection and validation. Based on the Law of Vibration, they will attract and gravitate toward other people and situations that give them a sense of certainty that they are loved.

If you do not have a high degree of self-worth, or you have been conditioned to look for love through other people or situations, then the last place you will look for love is in your own heart. In this case, you are more likely to believe that love is something that you get from other people by acting in a certain way or doing things in a certain way. Instead of seeing love as the mutual exchange of emotionally healthy people, it becomes horse trading. If you do "this" for me, then I will love you. If I do "that" for you, I am loving you. If we do "this" for each other, then we are loving each other. Sadly, when "this or that" disappears, so does the love.

For those that have this belief and act this way, it becomes easy to fall into emotionally unhealthy relationships where you are either abused, neglected or controlled, or you are the person causing the abuse, neglect or control. Some people do not get involved in unhealthy relationships. Instead, they look for the feeling of love through sex, shopping, food, drugs, or any of countless forms of emotional escapism that give them a temporary rush, which they can easily become addicted to as a "replacement" for love. They do this because in addition to having a need for love, we also have a need for certainty, which is the need for security, safety and comfort. This means that people will allow themselves a degree of pain or discomfort, or settle for less than what is ideal, in exchange for certainty, because the pain or discomfort that is predictable is safer than the uncertainty of the unknown.

People fall into this cultural pattern of horse-trading and looking outside of themselves for love because that is what is taught through TV, movies, magazines, books and other media and entertainment, and even religious institutions. None of these are self-love. They are emotional adaptations that are unsustainable and never lead to fulfillment. You cannot find self-love outside of yourself. You can never rely on someone else's love and validation of you to make you feel loved. You will always be disappointed.

When we are looking for love outside of ourselves, we will attract people for a variety of reasons. But the people that actually show up closest to us are based upon the strongest emotions that we are vibrating at the time. For example, if someone is afraid of betrayal, they are likely to attract someone who ends up doing something that makes them feel betrayed. If someone is ashamed of their body, they may attract someone who makes them feel shame. We are always drawing into our life people (and situations) that are a vibrational match.

People tend to show up in our life for either a specific reason or a season, and sometimes for a lifetime. Some people will show up because they bring us a lesson to learn or a perspective to gain. Others will only show up for a short season of time. But in that time we feel a powerful sense of love, connection, and validation and we will not want it to end. Some people want love so badly they will fall in love with anyone who makes them feel loved, significant, and validated. This type of volatile love is something to avoid. You do not want to create an image of someone as you want them to be, and then fall in love with the idea you projected onto the other person, rather than who they really are. If you do, you set yourself up for failure.

You always have to love yourself first and feel comfortable with who you are so that you develop the discernment to know who someone truly is in your life. You also have to learn how to let people go. If someone wants to walk out of your life, let them go, especially if you know you have done and been your best for them. You also have to know when to ask people to leave. You never want to keep people in your life who detract from your happiness. Nor do you want your own happiness to be dependent upon another person being in your life. Your own happiness and self-worth should come from within your own heart and be far more important than any one person in your life. Countless people will put up with tremendous amounts of fear and pain just to have someone say they love them. Do not be that person.

Using the analogy of a tree, there are three types of people who will enter our life. Some people are like leaves on a tree. When the wind blows they move in one direction and then the next. They take water and nutrients from the tree and give shade. When the seasons change, they whither up and die, and then they are gone from your life. Others are like branches. They are a large part of your life as long as it is convenient for them. When you have a challenge in your life and you ask to step out on their limb for assistance, they discard the relationship and go in another direction. Finally, there are people who are roots in your life. They are the ones who are always there for you during good times or bad. They are not swayed by the ups and downs of your life, and they are a reliable source of friendship, love, support, and encouragement. They know how to give and receive, they embrace you unconditionally, and they are a part of the fabric of your life. It is okay to have leaves and branches in your life. Sometimes they are very fun. Just do not expect them to act like roots, and make sure that they are not Vampires. It only takes a few solid roots to hold up an entire tree. Surround yourself with people who are roots because they will always be there to help you to learn and grow.

Self-love is about having deep roots and being the roots for other people. It begins with the first lesson in this book. Surround yourself with people you can learn from.

This lesson is a must. As Albert Einstein said, "We cannot solve problems using the same kind of thinking we used when we created them." In this case, if you want to learn how to love yourself and feel fulfilled, find people who are also committed to personal growth and are taking steps to enable their growth, and join in on their fun. You are not alone on an island. There are countless people in religious and spiritual organizations, social clubs, recreational or competitive sports, or any number of groups and activities who are excited about life and moving forward. Doing this is a big step in the right direction toward liberating yourself from being a slave to Vampires and putting you on the path of remembering your own self-worth.

When you are surrounded by people who share a passionate commitment around a common purpose, anything is possible.
-Howard Schultz

When you look at the big picture of how Dream Stealers shape your personality and Vampires hijack your life, it becomes clear that returning to a place of self-love is a choice, albeit not an easy one. When you make a decision to take ownership of your life, you are simultaneously making the choice to dismantle the web of unhealthy relationships and disempowering emotional habits that are associated with your past choices. The challenge with this is that at the moment of decision, the residue of your past does not disappear. It is not like all of the Vampires in your life suddenly vaporize, and all your bad habits and negative self-talk just vanish from your mind. They are all still there.

It is at the point of decision when you actually have to begin working on yourself and elevating your awareness of who you are and your capabilities. You have to develop the discernment to recognize the difference between challenges that represent residue from your past versus resistance from your choice to move in a new direction in life. With this discernment, you have to have a strategy that will allow you to mentally and emotionally separate the effects of your past from your new direction in life so as not to be distracted or derailed. You may still have to deal with and bring closure to events and circumstances from your past while at the same time forging ahead in a new direction. To do this you have to develop the skill of pattern recognition. This means recognizing when any negative, self-defeating thoughts or habits are coming up, what triggers them to come up, and knowing how to quickly replace them with a counter, positive intention. It also means becoming clear about the parts of your personal story that you are addicted to—the negative self-talk that you keep repeating to yourself—and finding a way to begin to change your inner-conversation, thoughts and beliefs, and their corresponding negative habits, into something self-empowering.

Unraveling your emotional entanglements and returning to a place of self-love takes discipline, and conscious, intentional work. It takes courage, inner-strength, perseverance and the willingness to push through the emotional pain that comes from letting go of emotional barriers. Just as a woman must push to give birth, you have to push past your fears and emotional barriers to learn and grow—even if the pushing and growth causes pain.

There are two types of pain—the pain that stops you and the pain that motivates you. Self-love is about the pain that motivates you. It is about recognizing that your subconscious mind is going to resist change at all costs by coming up with excuses not to do things or trying to reason itself out of taking new, unfamiliar action. The stronger your why—your action motivator for change—the faster and easier it will be to push yourself in a new direction.

When you look at the way your thoughts and beliefs are hard-wired into your brain and integrated into your subconscious mind, you begin to see that self-love is less about whether or not you want to love and accept yourself, and is more about breaking away from the shackles of mental programming that have kept you emotionally deprived. I do not know of anyone who does not want to love themselves or their own life. But I know of a lot of people who feel like they are constantly playing hide-and-go-seek with their own self-worth.

As you press forward in life, trying to find out who you are, what you want, and how to love yourself, it is easy to get lost behind the social pressures that want you to act or do things in a certain way as a prerequisite for being loved and accepted by others. And if you do not conform, you take the risk of being rejected. This type of social pressure has nothing to do with self-love, and it keeps you continuously looking outside of yourself for that perfect "something or someone" or the next best "thing" that will make you feel happy, significant, and loved. This seeking is rubbish. There is no place that you can go on this earth, nothing that you can eat, wear, purchase or do that will make you feel loved and accepted, other than going into your own heart and mind, and making peace with yourself as you are right now.

Even though "life" wants you to look outside yourself for love, there is little difference between what you experience outside of yourself and what is going on inside your heart and mind. Based on the Law of Vibration, the two are inseparable. Your outer world is an echo of your inner-world because your inner thoughts and beliefs determine how you see yourself, what you feel and the choices you make. These choices and feelings shape who and what you attract into your life. If you want to return to a place of living and enjoying your authentic, loving self and want to have an amazing, prosperous, fun-filled life, quit playing the game of charades with your heart and mind, and start being your genuine self.

It boils down to this: Self-love takes a do-or-die attitude. You have to be willing to let go of everything that is not working in your life—people, places and circumstance—and begin to surround yourself with people you can learn from and positive, uplifting people and situations that will raise your vibration and elevate you life experience. If you want to love yourself, let go of everything in your past that you associate with blame or pain that is holding you back, even if it hurts to do so. Forgive whoever needs to be forgiven, including yourself and put that baggage behind you. Make the tough decisions that will force you to grow and will enable you to let go of negative influences in your life. Then, take massive action to surround yourself with quality, loving, up-lifting people.

When you make the do-or-die decision to enter the path of self-love, none of your prior beliefs and experiences will go to waste. No matter what happened to you in your past, every thought, belief and experience can serve the purpose of self-love, if you let it. My close call with death did just that. It gave me the emotional leverage to make sense of my past and to develop my own view of self-love.

For me, self-love was the single most difficult challenge I ever gave myself. Coming from a childhood of mental and emotional abuse, being a runaway, and then encountering a close call with death was a lot of baggage to work through. Through all that, I learned the importance of living in a place of acceptance and allowance. This place is loving and accepting yourself just as you are, regardless of what you have gone through or are going through and without self-judgment. From there it requires having the courage to look into the fear and pain in the eyes of your Vampires and giggle at them as if they are clowns at a circus, knowing that they no longer have control over your life.

Self-love is being able to look in the mirror of your past, regardless of any undesirable or unfavorable life conditions and embrace the lessons from every hurt and pain, knowing that you are not your past, that you can learn from and be empowered by your story, and that you are fully capable of raising your personal standards and improving every aspect of your life. It is about having the strength to say yes to what you do want and no to what you do not want.

Self-love is self respect. It is never letting anyone look down on you or treat you in a manner that is degrading or demeaning. It is about setting mental and emotional boundaries so that no one ever again hijacks your heart and mind.

When faced with challenges, self-love is about standing up for yourself and what you believe and being a solid rock of confidence in the face of all adversity. You stand strong because you understand the power of thought and emotions, and you know how to use them with purpose and intention, rather than allowing your thoughts and emotions to use you.

Self-love is acknowledging that you, and you alone, are entirely responsible for every aspect of your life and that never again will you blame anyone for anything. As soon as a challenge shows up, the first thing you do is ask yourself one simple question: "What thoughts, feelings or beliefs do I have that caused me to attract this circumstance into my life?" Once you see the answer and you own it, then you face the problem and fix it.

Self-love is about waking up in the morning and feeling grateful for the life that you have. It is about treating yourself the way you want to be treated. It is about giving yourself gifts and experiences that raise your vibration and keep you in a place of joy and happiness. It is about doing things that put a smile on your face and keeping your mind stimulated and your heart fulfilled. It is about having love, romance, and affection in your life, music that you want to sing and dance to, and friends that make you smile and giggle.

Most importantly, self-love is about being in the flow of life. It is about giving and receiving. It is recognizing that each and every person on this planet, and all of life, is connected by a universal thread of energy. Self-love is being able to look at the person next to you or the person on the other side of the planet in an entirely different culture, and acknowledge that they are no less human than you. Self-love is having compassion for others. It is about contribution and growth and a willingness to do good for others because you understand that whatever you do to others you do to yourself.

The energy of self-love is contagious. Once you start walking with love in your heart, people will notice that there is something different about you. It will be in your eyes, your smile, and the way you walk and talk. You will begin to draw into your life people of like heart and mind, and the power of love will grow and expand.

When you love yourself, it is not just about having a confident, self-assured personality. It is also about owning and taking responsibility for your body—knowing that if you do not take care of you body, you have nowhere else to live. It is about understanding that your thoughts and feelings directly affect your health and so does the quality of the food that you put in your body, the water you drink, and the air you breathe. Knowing this, a big part of your confidence comes from having fun hobbies, regular exercise and activity, and eating foods that contribute to your overall well-being. These choices enable you to look in the mirror and love your body from the inside-out, regardless of any flaws, limitations or imperfections because you are not judging yourself for what you are not, but embracing what you are.

The rewards of self-love are immeasurable. Once you love your own life you tap into an unlimited reservoir of energy that gives you the resources to have, do and be anything you want. Most importantly, the energy of self-love projects onto all of life and becomes a magnetic force for attracting more goodness into your life.

Self-love is not a final destination. It is a feeling, an awareness, and a journey. And the secret to self-love is very simple: do whatever makes you feel loved. Surround yourself with beauty and with quality, uplifting friendships, and relationships. Immerse yourself in cultural experiences that will expand your view of life. Pamper yourself. Create a clean and peaceful home environment. Rest and rejuvenate regularly. Go for walks in nature. Walk barefoot on the grass. Get lots of sun. Play in the snow. Feed someone who is hungry. Exchange hugs and smiles. Express gratitude for what you have and give praise for other people's achievements. Giggle often and do whatever makes your heart sing. There is no greater experience in the world than to look at yourself with fresh eyes and an open heart, and to fall in love with yourself and life for the very first time.

Life is an inner journey disguised as outer experiences. Self-love is true freedom. Forgiveness is the doorway and gratitude is the key. For those that choose to stay committed to personal growth, self-love is the prize.

The person in life that you will always be with the most, is yourself. Because even when you are with others, you are still with yourself, too! When you wake up in the morning, you are with yourself, laying in bed at night you are with yourself, walking down the street in the sunlight you are with yourself. What kind of person do you want to walk down the street with? What kind of person do you want to wake up in the morning with? What kind of person do you want to see at the end of the day before you fall asleep? Because that person is yourself, and it is your responsibility to be that person you want to be with. I know I want to spend my life with a person who knows how to let things go, who's not full of hate, who's able to smile and be carefree. So that is who I have to be.
- C. JoyBell

It is Possible

Trust yourself.
Create the kind of self that you will be happy to live with all your life.
Make the most of yourself by fanning the tiny, inner sparks
of possibility into flames of achievement.
- Golda Meir

Everything in life is possible until proven otherwise.

You do not even have to be the same person tomorrow that you are today. All it takes is letting go and trying something new. As I learned through my own experience, personal transformation and self-love are a choice which must be followed up with faith, courage, and consistent action.

There are a lot of people who, when they look at the current conditions of their life can easily become overwhelmed with the amount of change that they must go through in order to rid themselves of their Vampires and elevate their self-worth. Although everyone's challenges are different and each person has different coping abilities, it is possible to transform your entire life. Countless people have already done so. They have overcome extreme disadvantages and are now living fully renewed and rejuvenated lives.

No matter what your age or life conditions, no matter what your childhood was like, or any undesirable circumstances that have shown up in your life, no matter how far you have fallen, all it takes is a change in perspective, courage, and action. It is possible, and if you believe it, then it can become your reality, too.

I am a product of believing in possibilities. The moment that I faced my own death I knew that I had nothing to lose if I put all my thought, energy, and emotion into saving my own life. Since death was already staring me in the face there was no risk in believing it was possible for me to survive and begin a new life. Not everyone will have the emotional leverage of a close call with death, but they can have their own version of do-or-die decision making.

If you are one of those people who is ready to transform your life, what if today was the day that you looked at your life and despite all unfavorable appearances, you chose to believe in possibilities?

What if today was the day that you were willing to become honest with yourself about the existence of the Energy Vampires in your life and the negativity of your own Inner Vampire, and you took immediate action to take complete ownership of your life?

What if today was the day that you gathered up the courage and you declared this moment to be a turning point in your life, and everything began to change and you accepted it and allowed it?

What if today was the day that you finally looked in the mirror and realized how beautiful and powerful you are?

What if today was the day that you finally realized that you have deep inside you, deep inside your heart and mind, all the love, strength, courage, and determination that you need to overcome any obstacle, pursue any dream and be the person you are fully capable of being?

What if today was the day that you finally let go of all your excuses, all your petty distractions, all your senseless blame, and finally began to love and accept yourself just as you are?

What if today was the day that, regardless of where you are in your life, you drew a line in the sand, mustered up all your courage, and raised your standards in every area of your life?

What if today was the day that once and for all you said no to what you do not want and yes to what you do want?

What if today was the day that you fell in love with yourself and no longer needed the validation of others?

What if today was the day that you allowed true love into your life—for yourself and for another?

What if today was the day that you finally realized and accepted that none of us are perfect; we all have strengths and weaknesses, and you learned to truly accept yourself and others?

What if today was the day that you finally realized that this event that we call our lifetime will not go on forever, and that the most important thing is to experience true happiness and true love?

What if today was the day that you gave yourself permission to pursue your dreams without fear of failure, and you did so in spite of any perceived obstacles or other people's opinions?

What if this moment right now was the point of intersection in time where your dreams actually started becoming a reality?

What if this was actually the moment, and you finally paid attention, took action, and your life began to change?

If today was the day, what would your new life look like and feel like?

Today can be that day. Today can be the day that you declare, once and for all, that you own your life and that you are going to do anything and everything you can to wean yourself off your past hurts and pains, shed your Vampires, and begin living your dreams.

In a world filled with overwhelming negativity, you are still allowed to create and live in your own oasis of happiness. You are allowed to feel completely blessed and overjoyed with your life, and grateful for every miracle that you experience, even if others live in misery. You do not need anyone's permission to be yourself, to be happy or to feel loved. You only need your own permission. You do not need to fit in and be accepted by others. You only need to accept yourself.

There is only a limited amount of time to live the rest of your life. You have no idea when you will breathe your last breath, cry your last tear, smile your last smile, or giggle your last giggle. Do not assume that you will have tomorrow, because tomorrow is never promised. You will always have more dreams than you will have time for them to come true. Decide what is most important to you in life, and make it your purpose and passion. Let today be the day that you believe in possibilities, and you begin to live your life with love.

IT IS possible!

BE HAPPY

Happiness cannot be traveled to, owned, earned, worn or consumed.
Happiness is the spiritual experience of living every minute with
love, grace, and gratitude.
- Denis Waitley

Now that you have learned about your Dance With Vampires are you ready to be happy?

One of the most rewarding parts of life is personal growth, and seeing the results of that growth manifest themselves in your life. Even better is when your growth leads to a realization about life that is so profound that you burst into uncontrolled giggles of happiness.

My realization occurred the moment I truly understood that our thoughts are magnets, and consistent thoughts, feelings, and choices shape our reality. Our life experiences are truly a mirror and echo of our innermost beliefs. The more I have come to understand this truth, the happier and freer I have become.

Life is so simple compared to how complicated we make it. When I first became aware of the truth that the secret to returning to your natural state of happiness is as simple as surrounding yourself with happy people and doing things that you enjoy, I also realized the incredible value that our Vampires serve toward our happiness.

How do Vampires contribute to you being happy? It is very simple. You gain experience and awareness through contrast. Sometimes, in order to discover who you are, you must first experience who you are not. It is the Law of Polarity. Everything exists in terms of its opposite. You cannot hide from this truth. Life will present countless opportunities to experience this contrast—to either love yourself and express your happiness or question your own value and self-worth. The challenge is when you get lost in the contrast and never embrace the lessons that it has to offer. This "getting lost" is when your life becomes consumed by Vampires.

As you go through life and live this contrast, you will dance with Vampires and you will also find yourself with many wonderful people. Through each of these dances you will accumulate a collage of memories and emotions. Of the many things you accumulate, there are only two things that you will leave behind that are of any lasting value—your relationships and the memory of how you lived your life. Both of these are predicated upon the relationship you have with yourself.

There is no more important relationship than the one you have with yourself. It is one of learning and growing, advancing and retreating, loving and being loved, giving and receiving, rejecting and being rejected, forgiving and being forgiven. In it you will experience deep pain and the joy of tremendous gain.

Your relationship with yourself starts out each morning when you wake up and ends when you go to sleep. How you start each day—from your first thoughts upon waking, through your last thoughts before you go to bed, are what determines the quality of your life. The ideal life is to work through the contrast so that you can experience your true nature as a being of love and happiness and to enjoy the journey.

Happiness is a choice. No matter where your path takes you, always keep in mind the simple truth that you are responsible for your own happiness. It is not something that can be given to you. True happiness—that deep inner giggle and smile that comes from a healthy outlook on life—is a gift that only you can give to yourself. It comes from self-love and from complete ownership of your thoughts, feelings, actions, and beliefs.

Life offers many gifts. Some we give, some we receive. There is no greater gift or accomplishment than to be happy with yourself and your life. Once you connect within your own heart to the happiness that you seek, you will encounter even greater reasons to fully embrace life and all its beauty.

No matter where your path takes you always keep in mind the

simple truth that you have within your very own heart and mind the keys to happiness—the tools to craft the reality of your choosing. The only restriction is time. You do not have forever. As eternal as a lifetime may seem, it can end at any moment, without warning. Once it ends, if you have not learned how to liberate yourself from the darkness of your Vampires and to connect with the joy that can be found in your own heart, you will have missed out on the most magnificent gift imaginable.

Never give up on happiness. As long as you are still alive, regardless of how things appear in the moment, there is always a road ahead. You do not have to spend your entire life Dancing With Vampires. Each moment is a fresh opportunity to begin life anew. There will always be opened doors ahead. When one door begins to close, it is only because that experience no longer serves your higher good and it has given you a sign that you are ready to move in a different direction in life. If you are not living your life's purpose, or your life is consumed by the toxicity of Vampires, doors will begin to close simply because they are guiding you to change direction. If you do not pay attention to the signs, those signs will become louder and louder, until you are "painfully ejected" from your current reality and forced into a new direction...until you have some type of "rock" experience that forces you to change.

Let the experience of my rock be your guide. Pay attention to your thoughts and feelings and to the events that are showing up in your life. Pay attention to the pains, failures, and setbacks. Many of the experiences that show up in your life may be signs that you are ready for change. If your approach to life is not working, if it does not bring you happiness, reach deep into the roots of your heart and mind and release the mental and emotional charade that has cast a shadow over your life.

Life is finite. It is meant to be enjoyed. Do not take this moment, or anyone you love, for granted. Do not cling to the past. It is nothing but an anchor that prevents you from moving forward.

Allow your heart and mind to be free. Set your vision forward. With all your strengths and weaknesses, be excited about who you are.

Be happy. Embrace all that life has to offer. When faced with difficult decisions, remember that the only things we ever have to hold onto are the things we are afraid to let go of.

Pay attention to your feelings. Before you take action give thought to the potential outcomes of different choices.

Listen to other people. Listen to their words and feelings. Be present when in the company of others.

Show compassion—for yourself, for others, for nature and humanity.

Connect with your feelings. Tap into the energy of emotions.

Contribute to the well-being of your friends, family, community, and humanity. Give for the sake of giving. Not because you want something in exchange.

Find beauty and laughter in the moment. Move quickly from pain and sorrow to happiness and gratitude.

Communicate clearly and speak with integrity. Say only what you mean. Replace negative self-talk about yourself and others with words that will grow goodness, prosperity, and community.

Say "no" to that which will weaken you, including your own self-limiting thoughts and beliefs. Say "yes" to that which will give you inner-strength and self-respect.

Love yourself and others as a genuine expression of your own self-love.

Respect and take care of your body. Eat properly and give your body the exercise and nutrients it is hungry for.

Forgive yourself for your shortcomings. Release yourself from the emotional shackles of blame and forgive others.

Be a self-reliant team player. Surround yourself with positive, uplifting people who will encourage you and aid you in the pursuit of your dreams.

Utilize the seven laws and the faculties of the mind with purpose and intention. They are here to help you move forward.

Be authentic. Be your true-self from the inside-out.

Be at peace with life, with the moment, and with the endless changes that come forth each day.

Dance and celebrate the many small gifts that come with each moment in time.

Elevate the vibration of your thoughts and feelings and live in a place of joy and love.

Pay attention to the thoughts you are broadcasting. They are the reality that you are creating and attracting, and the preview of coming attractions.

Giggle at yourself and the simplicity and silliness of life.

Love yourself unconditionally. When you do, you will impact all of humanity, and will have a love affair that will last for eternity.

Get out of line. Stop waiting. You do not need a reason to be happy. The time to be happy is now.

Take responsibility for your life. Look back on your life experiences as lessons in a classroom. But this time, let it be up to you to decide the meaning you give to your experiences.

Learn from your past. Gain a new perspective and make new, healthier choices for future actions.

Live with courage. Be honest and truthful, with yourself and others. Contribute to our world in a positive and meaningful way.

Live from the heart. Live with passion. Live with purpose.

Honor those you love. Give your energy to that which creates beauty and gives light to life.

Above all, live in a place of Gratitude, Love, and Giggles.

I am going to be happy.
I am going to skip. I am going to be glad.
I am going to smile a lot.
I am going to be easy. I am going to count my blessings.
I am going to look for reasons to feel good.
I am going to dig up positive things from the past.
I am going to look for positive things where I stand.
I am going to look for positive things in the future.
It is my natural state to be a happy person.
It is natural for me to love and to laugh.
This is what is most natural for me.
I am a happy person!
- Esther Hicks

THE BIG PICTURE

Waking up is not a selfish pursuit of happiness,
it is a revolutionary stance, from the inside out,
for the benefit of all beings in existence.
- Noah Levine

Up until now I have addressed our Dance With Vampires on a personal level, and I have presented the seven lessons in a way that will allow you to work on your own personal development. Let's step back now and look at the bigger picture of life and magnify the importance of returning to a place of self-love.

When I first started exploring the lessons presented from the rock to my head, I initially saw it as a personal wake-up call for my own life. But after learning the seven lessons and noticing the rapid changes in my own life, it has grown into a broader vision for wanting to have a meaningful impact on all of humanity. I now see that our Dance with Vampires is not exclusively an individual experience. Nor is it an analogy for just your own personal growth. It has also become a way to bring light to the collective experience of all of humanity.

Now, more than ever, the vast majority of humanity is Dancing with Vampires. While it is true that we all awaken to our own heart potential at our own pace, and have the right to live in our own oasis of happiness, this does not negate the importance of each of us waking up to the reality that the entire planet has been overtaken by Vampires.

When you peel away the distractions of day-to-day-life, and the filtered reality presented by the media, it is clear that there is a mental and emotional dis-ease of pandemic proportions that is causing us to destroy ourselves and is simultaneously destroying the hearts and lives of billions of people across the globe. The amount of personal suffering on this planet is so vast that it has become all too easy to emotionally distance ourselves from it, and accept it as an unfortunate, but normal part of the human experience. The reality is that most people on the planet are severely deprived of love, self-worth and the basic necessities of life. This deprivation is the effect of the battle with our global Dance with Vampires.

Given the amount of resources on this planet, there is no reason for anyone to live in deprivation of the basic necessities of life. There is no reason to raise children in fear and to perpetuate the lie of learned helplessness and victim-consciousness. There is no reason for people to live in filth and disease. There is no reason other than we have been purposefully kept in the dark about who we are and what we are capable of, and have never been introduced to our true power. We have forgotten that we are a part of nature, not apart from it, because through cultural, social and religious influences we have been overtaken by Vampires and distracted from the truth.

It is easy to see the effects that Vampirism has had on the planet. We have caused a lot of destruction that has now become so obvious that most of the world is trying to figure out what happened and how we got here. We are looking at our world with shock, tears and disgust, trying to figure out what to do to restore the planet and our own hearts to their natural place of peace, love, and harmony. With so many people looking for a place to point blame, we should each be pointing to ourselves because individually and collectively, we are responsible for the condition of our planet through our own choices.

Realistically, there are only several thousand world leaders who run this planet and control the lives of billions of people. Although some people would want to blame world governments, and other political social and religious organizations for keeping us locked into socio-economic systems that leave us entrenched in financial scarcity, fear, and emotional deprivation, we are not victims of these institutions. They are a reflection of our collective mental and emotional reality. Knowing the laws of vibration and attraction, and how our thoughts and feelings shape our reality, it is easy to understand that humanity is having this global experience because we have drawn it into our reality due to the fact that the collective thought and emotional vibration of humanity is stuck in fear and scarcity, and misguided by the false belief that we are energetically separate from each other and from all of life. We are perpetuating our own alienation and destruction through choice, neglect or ignorance.

Although this problem has been going on throughout recorded history, we are reaching a crescendo of poverty, disease, and planetary destruction that may be irreversible—unless we wake up and start acting like a global community instead of a handful of individuals pursuing their own interests and fighting amongst each other over petty differences. All of the pushing-against each-other, resisting and judging only perpetuates fear and scarcity and further advances the destruction of our planet.

Even though we are here to have our own unique journey, the time has come for us to wake up and accept the simple truth that we are vibrational beings, and we are all connected. We can no longer pretend to be ignorant of this fact. We are equally responsible for our own choices, and for the effect that our choices have on each other and on our planet. We cannot bomb one part of the earth and not have it affect the entire planet. We cannot pollute the oceans, lakes, and rivers and not have it affect the food that we eat and water that we drink. We get what we give.

Having now taken a snapshot of the big picture of life, all of this is good news. What works on the personal level also works on a global level. Just as we individually gain experience through contrast, and this gives us the emotional leverage to create change in our own life, this also happens on a global level. We, as a species, are given the opportunity to regain our power by reaching a threshold of suffering. Once we cross that threshold and can no longer tolerate the pain—that is when we will shed our Vampires, drop our masks, discard our differences and reunite as a global community.

How can this happen? Vampires are afraid of love. They feed on fear and scarcity. Until such a time that we stop feeding them they will continue to control our lives so long as we give them permission to do so by us remaining ignorant and asleep. However, one-by-one, as each of us sheds our Vampires, takes responsibility for our own lives, and learns how to again listen to our heart and use our mind, that is when we will return to a place of self-love.

Vampires are the problem. Awareness is the solution. It starts in our own heart and mind, then expands outwardly into our family, community, nation and global community. It begins when we realize that we live in an abundant universe with an infinite supply of energy and resources to create anything that wants to be created. It begins with simple coffee-talk amongst friends and family. It begins when we meet our neighbors and create a sense of belonging by doing things together to improve our neighborhood. It begins when we start being friendly with the people with whom we interact on a daily basis. It begins when we look at what we have in common rather than at what separates us. It begins when we make better choices about the food we eat and the products we consume and discard. It begins when we pay attention to our thoughts, feelings, and beliefs, pulling the weeds of negativity and sowing new, positive, and empowering ideas. It begins when we discard our self-limiting, self-defeating story and create a new, empowering reality. It begins when we realize that behind every set of eyes is the same power and force that created each of us. Behind every set of eyes is an individualized expression of the entire fabric of energy and life.

Our Dance with Vampires will end when we realize that we are the solution. Our solutions start with gratitude, forgiveness and accepting responsibility for ourselves.

They begin right here, right now by taking action.

- Get off your ass and do something different
- Surround yourself with people you can learn from
- Be honest with yourself and others
- Face your problems head on and solve them
- Pay attention to your thoughts and feelings before they become your reality
- Learn from your past and replace blame with self-responsibility.
- Show gratitude and be forgiving
- Give people reasons to love themselves
- Remain open-minded and teachable
- Pay attention to your Vampires. They are showing you where you are weak and ready to learn and grow
- Surround yourself with people who can help make you strong
- Shy away from negativity and open up to enthusiasm
- Do at least one thing every day for yourself that makes you feel amazing

- Do something every day that helps someone without expecting anything in return
- Pray for others. Give thanks for your blessings
- Giggle out loud and giggle often

EPILOGUE

How Did I Get Here?

Coaches, Volleyball & Puppies

It is always important to know when something has reached its end.
Closing circles, shutting doors, finishing chapters, it does not matter
what we call it; what matters is to leave in the past
those moments in life that are over.
- Paulo Coelho, The Zahir

When I set out to write this book, it was because I believed that it is possible for people to transform their entire life, regardless of circumstances. I believe it is possible because I have been doing it myself. Each of the seven lessons that I shared has worked for me and are now an integral part of my daily approach to life. They can work for you too, as long as you further explore the ideas and put them to practical use.

Although I have come a long way since my date with that rock, there is a lot further I want to go in my personal development. My real growth started to begin in October of 2013 when I made a big leap of faith and returned to society.

After nearly four years of living with family near my hometown of Telluride, Colorado and healing my wounds I began mustering up the courage to resume my life. I made several trips to Boulder (where I had gone to college at the University of Colorado) to test the waters. My dear friend Micah, who I had grown up with in Telluride, gave me the final nudge and took me into his home in Boulder and helped me to re-adjust to society. My first book, which Micah had read, had a positive impact on his life and he was returning the favor by helping me out, as any good friend would. Since I had mostly isolated myself while I was recovering in Telluride, I lost perspective of how much my life had decayed in those four years until I made it back to Boulder. My self-image and athleticism were subpar and I had forgotten how to socialize. I felt emotionally defeated and disconnected from daily life. I needed the leverage of a good friend to help me remember who I am and what I am capable of accomplishing.

At that point in time, since I had already written and released my first book, Footsteps After The Fall, I spent a lot of my time pounding the pavement, doing book signings and small speaking engagements. But it was a struggle. Having been given a second chance at life gave me a lot of ambition and enthusiasm for wanting to make a difference in people's lives, but my self-image did not yet fit my ambitions. It was then that I realized that I had a lot more work to do on myself than I had realized.

When it comes to starting your life all over again, there are not any hard and fast rules about where to go or what to do first. Some people find religion. Others find fitness, sports, or spirituality. I chose a starting point that was familiar and had no downside. I began the uphill climb of restoring my body by working out daily and eating only organic foods. I knew that if I restored my overall health, wellness, and fitness, my mind would follow. I also knew that I had to surround myself with people that I could learn from, so while working out at the gym I began listening to audio books by some of my favorite mentors and teachers, and I flooded my mind with positive, uplifting, and inspiring messages on a daily basis. Knowing that gratitude erases negativity, I also did everything I could to focus on what I was grateful for in my life. With Micah continuing to nudge me to get out more often and meet people, I slowly regained my edge on life.

Reestablishing myself in society was one of the greatest challenges I had ever given myself. It would have been much easier to stay where I was and let time take its course. But there was a fire inside me that could not be blown out. Almost losing my life is what actually gave me life.

With each day that I moved forward, I became relentlessly focused on rebuilding the foundation of my physical, mental and emotional health, and launching a whole new life for myself. I started getting unexpected phone calls and emails from people who had read my book—telling me how it had changed their life. Then, through a twist in fate, in 2013 I met a Life Coach. I told her my personal story, and her first response was, "you have an important message that you need to share with others." She then gave me the gift of one year of Life Coaching. I graciously accepted.

I was given two Life Coaches, Cheri and Marilyn, and another Coach/Accountability Partner, Annelise, and that is when my life truly began to change at hyper speed. Life Coaches are not mentors or therapists, and they do not give advice. Rather, in the same way that an athletic coach helps an athlete improve their game by helping them to fine tune their skills, a Life Coach is trained to help you clean up your thinking, overcome self-limiting beliefs, gain a deeper sense of purpose, set goals and create an action plan. Life Coaches can help you find mentors, and navigate your way toward your sweet spot goals and life purpose so that you can more quickly and easily accomplish them.

For me, having two life coaches and an accountability partner did all the above and more. Cheri, Marilyn and Annelise also recognized the value of my life experience and they helped me to piece my life back together in a very strong, loving and methodical way. They gave me the emotional leverage to believe in myself again. Whatever goals I set, they helped me to become clear about what I wanted and when, and they showed me that it is possible.

Although at the time I had thought that pursuing my passion of making a difference in people's lives was my priority, my coaches helped to see more clearly that my sweet spot goal was to find my own place to live and get physically settled. Within 11 months of my first day of receiving coaching I was able to move into a beautiful loft in Denver. Almost five years from the date of my injury I was finally on my own again and I began the journey of re-socializing myself and finding my place in society.

When you are starting your life over again, and committed to doing the work on yourself to learn and grow, a lot of miracles happen. As part of my recovery, I had given away all of my furniture. My first personal goal was to purchase some furniture. By some miracle, on the day I moved in, one of the neighbors was moving out and they had a bunch of furnishing that they did not want to put in storage. They gave me a fridge full of organic food, a bed, desk, chairs, cleaning supplies, and a case of hand crafted beer. When events like that happen, you know that you are thinking clearly, that your heart and vibration are in the right place, and you are moving in the right direction. When I went to bed on that first night, I cried myself to sleep with tears of gratitude.

Beyond getting furniture, my B.A.G. (Big Ass Goal) was to be happy. I wanted to savor my second chance at life, try new things, experience true love and feel vibrant and alive.

Moving to the city had the same feeling of unfamiliarity as arriving in a foreign country for the first time. Being a mountain guy, I was accustomed to living a daily lifestyle of rock and ice climbing, hiking, camping, mountaineering, boarding, and skiing, and having the beauty and fresh air of the mountains as my home turf. City life is very different. It has a pulse and cadence that was unfamiliar. At first, I definitely felt like a social outcast. I found it very difficult to break free from my "mountain mindset." Yet I pushed myself forward and embraced the unfamiliarity as an opportunity to challenge myself to learn and grow and expand my view of life. Soon after my move to the city, I began seeking out ways to meet people, socialize, go on dates, and have fun. Instead of looking for new friends who were active in independent sports, I decided to find a different tribe of friends by picking up a team sport that I had not played yet, that would challenge me physically, mentally, and socially. Volleyball became my new love.

Volleyball is one of the most sexy, social, and athletic team sports around. It quickly became a great way for me to meet people and regain my edge as an athlete. I immediately jumped in and started playing indoor, sand, and grass volleyball. I had no idea what I was doing, but I did not care. I just immersed myself in the sport and figured I would learn it as I played. Socially, it is off the charts fun. Physically, it showed me how much more work I had to do on my mind and body. It was rough being new to a sport, but I was totally up for pushing myself in a new direction. I have since played in six mountain tournaments and in a week long beach tournament in Ixtapa, Mexico. I also played in a MUDD Volleyball tournament as a benefit for March of Dimes. It was big fun. Volleyball has become a regular part of my everyday life, and it keeps my soul happy. I still have a long way to go to reach a more competitive level, but I found my home socially and athletically, and I am loving the journey of continuously meeting new people and growing as an athlete.

In keeping with my goal to do and enjoy whatever makes me happy and to stay emotionally healthy, I decided to bring an animal companion into my life that would give me a sense of joy, purpose, and responsibility outside of myself. You have not lived or loved until you have adopted a puppy. I cannot think of a single thing that has brought more happiness and joy into my life than the newness of a puppy and the loyal, unconditional love of a dog. I adopted a Stabyhoun and named her Finnley. Since the day I picked her up she has been a breath of fresh air and has brought joy and emotional stability to my life. Emotional companions are invaluable to post-trauma people like me who are re-adapting to a new life. Finnley has reminded me how much fun it is to be new at life and how exciting it can be to be teachable. Puppy energy gets you up early, keeps you up late, and keeps you active. Finnley is an exceptionally loving and intelligent dog who continuously challenges me to get out of my head and into my heart. You can follow Finnley on her public Facebook page where she shares morsels of happiness and wisdom.

www.Facebook.com/FinnleyKisses

I have so much to be grateful for in my life. In the two years since I moved to Denver I have had an amazing restart to my life. I have pushed myself to learn and grow in so many different directions and have done my best to meet my challenges with strength and courage and stay true to the seven lessons that became the framework for my new life.

Slaying my own Vampires and rebuilding my life from ground-zero has not been an easy endeavor. I have had to constantly face the backlash of the physical and emotional residue of my past while at the same time digging deeply for the courage to move forward. I would not have been able to make it were it not for the support of an army of friends who love and encourage me.

Through all of this, I have one friend who has stood out as a shining star. Special thanks to my dear friend Barb, who has been the backbone of my new life. Barb has been a miraculous friend and the creative heart and mind behind giving my story a visual and global presence.

When I look at where I am now, in the very center of my dreams quickly becoming a reality, I can see how receiving coaching was the game changer for me and is what has brought all this together. I have developed such a strong belief in the seven lessons and the value of having a coach that I have now entered the profession of being a life results coach and a professional transformational speaker. I have found so much joy in the dance with my Vampires that I have developed a deep enthusiasm for helping others to slay their own Vampires and realize their dreams.

As I move forward with my journey of applying the seven lessons in my own life, I am working diligently to leverage my Rock Story by sharing these lessons worldwide through the development and launch of The Giggle Yoga Project.

Giggle Yoga is the Yoga of being happy. It is the daily practice of owning your life, being mentally and emotionally flexible, and living with gratitude, forgiveness, and self-responsibility.

The purpose of the Giggle Yoga Project is to help people reconnect with their happiness through professional speaking engagements, coaching services, and workshops, and other tools and resources that empower, motivate, inspire and encourage. It is the platform through which I am sharing the gift of the seven lessons as an author, transformational speaker, and life results coach.

Life gave me a second chance. I am grateful for my Dance With Vampires because through all my pain and suffering I have become clear about what I am not, and re-discovered who I am and why I am here.

Let us all now Dance with Love, Gratitude and Giggles.

Namaste!

Acknowledgements

Life is a team sport. We are all here for each other. I extend my deepest gratitude to a handful of close friends and family who have loved me and supported me throughout my life. In the tree of my life they are the roots which have helped me to keep myself alive and to thrive. I love each of you very deeply.

Marianne Jacqueline Strauss, My beautiful Mom: Though my mom died during my youth, I am grateful for the gift of life that she gave me. I will always cherish the memories I do have of her. There is no doubt in my heart and mind that my mother would love me just the way I am and that she would have supported and encouraged me in all my adventures and journeys. I continue to think about her each and every day of my life and have always kept a picture of her with me wherever I am. I truly love and appreciate my mom and thank her for watching over me all these years.

Juliette Strauss, Sister: There is only one person who has been with me since the day I was born: my sister, Juliette. There is no doubt that the illness and death of our mom had a lasting impact on both our lives. Yet against all odds, we have both become stronger through the challenges presented by life. Through good times and bad, and all the ups and downs, we have always grown stronger and closer. I am endlessly grateful for her on-going love and support, and for keeping me on my toes throughout my life. She is a tremendously courageous, caring, and loving lady with a deep sense of humor. She has always loved me and accepted me as I am. I love Juliette with all my heart and soul. Always have and always will!

Arthur Strauss, Father: Words can never describe my father. He is one of the most interesting, loving, adventurous people I have ever met. Now 90 years young, he continues to yodel, walk, hike and ride his bicycle. He views life with an open heart and an abundance of happiness. He laughs more than anyone I know, and he can find adventure in the joy of world travels or the simplicity of watching a ladybug walk across a flower petal. He gave me and my sisters and brother life, and he has brought a tremendous amount of joy and hope into other people's lives. He is a true Giggle Yoga Warrior. I love and appreciate my dad, and I am forever grateful for the example of health and vitality he has brought into my life.

Cathrin Strauss, Mom # 2: Cathrin came into my life through her marriage to my father. I was the unexpected gift she received as a result of my mother's illness and death. I could not have asked for a more perfect second mother than Cathrin. From the first day we met, she always treated me like I was her own son and continued to touch my life with the wings of an angel. She always did her best to love and inspire me and was the glue that kept my sense of hope alive. Cathrin also passed away too young, but she left behind the beautiful legacy of my sister Amanda, and the memory of her gentle, creative and caring heart. I will always love and appreciate Cathrin.

Amanda Strauss, Sister: When I was 21, I went on a ten-month journey across Australia and New Zealand. On March 10th, 1986, while in Lilydale, Australia, my dad called to tell me that I now had a new sister. Life has never been the same. Amanda has been a barrel of fun ever since she came into my life. From the first time I took her fishing to the gifts of watching her grow up and get married, she has been an incredible sister and someone I love and care for deeply and joyfully. Amanda and I share the same father. Amanda's mother is Cathrin.

Jordan Strauss Ancel, Brother: Jordan is five years younger than I am. We grew up in different households but spent enough time together to feel a brotherly bond of love and respect. No matter how far apart we may have been in distance, he has always shown his love and support. He has an incredibly healthy outlook on life and has an enormous amount of personal courage and inner strength. I definitely have lots of love and gratitude for my brother! Jordan and I share the same father. Jordan's mother, Teresa, is also someone I love and appreciate.

Barbara Wade, Dear Friend: Having met Barbara is proof of the law of vibration and attraction. Through an unusual string of events, which could be a book all its own, Barbara came into my life and has been the creative heart and spirit that has given my ambitions a digital presence. Barbara is a creative and loving person who knows how to receive by giving. Thank you Barbara for all your love and support in bringing The Giggle Yoga Project to life. Love, Gratitude, and Giggles to you and SAM.

Michael Cordova, Dear Friend: Mike is one of the most beautiful, loving, caring people to enter into my life. We have built a rock-solid friendship since the day we first met. If there has ever been a person who has been consistently enthusiastic about life and learning, it's Mike. Anyone who has a chance to get to know him will be truly blessed. He is my best friend, and I am truly grateful for the deep, loving friendship we share. His brother, parents and relatives are so close to my heart that they feel like family.

Kelly Straeter, Dear Friend: Kelly has been there for me in so many different ways and has always brought joy, humor, laughter and love into my life. I truly love, respect and appreciate Kelly for the unique gift she has been in my life. She is one of the most sincere, generous, beautiful, funny and real people I have ever met. She has a uniquely charming approach to life, and a strong and gentle heart.

Michael Weiner, Dear Friend: Michael has been my father's friend longer than I have been alive. He is a pillar of wisdom and practicality and has been an incredible source of encouragement and support. He is someone I look up to for his personal and professional achievements and for his generous and caring heart. He has been a strong role-model in my life, and someone that I appreciate, love, and respect.

Autumn Riddle, Dear Friend: I met Autumn while I was living in Yuma, Arizona. Autumn is a rare, beautiful and gentle soul with a deep, loving and caring heart. She is far more than a wonderful artist. She is someone who cares deeply about others and is a true blessing to anyone she gets close to. Autumn has touched my heart and my life with kindness and gentleness. I have a deep love and respect for Autumn.

Mike Maish, Dear Friend: Mike has been a true friend on every level of life. I extend my deepest gratitude for his genuine support during my college and post-graduate years. In more ways than one, Mike has been a powerful pillar of support throughout my journey. Mike has tremendous heart and integrity and is a living demonstration of the power of love and forgiveness.

Kristi Lyn Gall, Dear Friend: Kristi and I go back to our teenage years in Telluride. She has been a consistent friend and an incredible mirror for my thoughts, ideas and emotions. We have a very intuitive connection and have had many parallel life experiences. No matter where each of us is in our lives, we can always count on each other for genuine friendship and support. Kristi is definitely someone that I love and care about and am grateful to have in my life.

Drew Juen, Dear Friend: Drew has been a true and genuine friend. He has shown up during the best and worst of times and has been consistently honest and genuine. He has incredibly strong character and rock-solid integrity. We have been through quite a few life experiences together and have helped each other to learn and grow. I am truly thankful for his friendship. Drew is someone that I appreciate and respect, and love as a brother.

"Aloha" Ardath Michael, Dear Friend: Aloha is a master of happiness. She is a beautiful, loving, caring lady with a depth of spiritual insight and awareness that is truly healing and encouraging. When we met at Deanza Springs Resort, we became instant friends. She is a spiritual sister and a true beacon of light to everyone that meets her. She brings to the moment a bouquet of love and joy and is an inspiration to everyone. I have a deep love and appreciation for our friendship.

Micah Page, Dear Friend: If it weren't for Micah, I would probably still be hiding in the mountains. Anyone who is fortunate enough to have Micah as a friend knows that he has rock-solid integrity which comes from his strong commitment to personal growth. Micah is very intuitive and insightful, and has the keen ability to dissect ideas into their most simple form. Some of my best conversation about life and ideas are with Micah. I am truly grateful for our authentic, loving friendship.

Arthur Cranstoun, Dear Friend: No matter where I am in my life's journey, Arthur is always in the background as a reliable source of love, support and encouragement. Just as he does with everyone he meets, Arthur has brought unconditional love, humor, and goodness to my life. He is someone whom I love and care for, and am truly grateful to call a friend.

Hawkwind Soaring, Godfather: When I moved on my own at age sixteen I met a wizard named Hawkwind. I refer to him as my godfather because, from the day I first met him, he has treated me like his own son and has supported me and guided me during my best and worst times. Hawkwind came into my life during a very vulnerable time for me. My mother had passed away. I was living on my own, seeking answers that would make sense of my life. He introduced me to the path of self-awareness and self-discovery. He planted seeds in my mind that allowed me to go through life seeing myself as a spiritual being having a human experience, rather than a human being having a spiritual experience.

Special Thanks to the following businesses for their loyal support:

Albert Roer:	TellurideProperties.com
Bob Franzese:	BlackBearTrading.com
Greg & Colleen Doudt:	SanJuanLiquors.com
Jon Terry:	AlarisProperties.com
Justin Abrams:	GreatScottsEatery.com
Lee Zeller:	VacationTelluride.com
Nels Cary:	TellurideSothebys.com
Randy Hancock:	RandysAutoCare.com
Ray Bowers:	RealEstateInTelluride.net
Tom Mortell:	TimberlineAceHardware.com

Also, I want to give thanks to the following people who have been an important part of my life over the past two years. Of course, there are countless others who have left a lasting impression upon my heart and mind: Amber Waits, Amy Taylor, Bob Boggs, Brian Bonds, Christopher Leach, Coral Grant, Cynthia Signet, Dale Aychman, Danny Hirsch, David Corbin, David Smith, Daria and Michael Bugg, Dianna Vaughn, Eric Trujillo, Erika Jiménez, Gene Duggan, Gerry Gruber, Gregory Kowalik, Greg Seeligson, Imo Sharman, Jim Looney, John Napoli, Jackie and Chuck Arguelles, Diana Fisher, James McCutcheon, Jessica Robbins, Jill Rosen, Laura Lagos, Levi Hernandez, Ligia Ramírez Steller, Marcelee Gralaap, Mimi Newstadt, Myra Hunter, Nancy Alterman, Amalia Maloney, Patsy & Anthony Cordova, Richard Millard, Ryan Wipf, Sandy Brown, Sheri Sharman, Tony Trello, Tracy Jacobsen, Valan Cain, Will Clark, Zeneida Fernández Roja.

Special thanks to my volleyball friends who embraced me as a new player and welcomed me in to the volleyball crowd. Brandon Kull, Brian Forte, Bruno Echegoyen, Dominick Bass, Kent Schmeckpeper, Kris Bradehoft, Kyle Cox, Lizzy Card, Nicholas & Mary Jo Henry, Tara Sindylek, Wade Bass.

Finally, none of this would have been possible if it hadn't been for that silly rock, to which I owe my deepest debt of gratitude.

That rock changed my life. Hopefully, it has changed yours too!

COMMENTS FROM READERS OF DAVID'S FIRST BOOK ~FOOTSTEPS AFTER THE FALL~

Order the book online at FootstepsAfterTheFall.com

"After reading Footsteps After The Fall, I thought to myself... ."Get this book and information to the graduating Seniors at Telluride High School!" As they transition into fresh lives outside of our tiny valley, what a better send off than having David's meaningful words go with them. I was on a mission... .and succeeded! At graduation, every senior got the book signed by David with a powerful message to each one of them. Thank you, David, from my heart for making this happen!"

Lee Zeller - Telluride, Colorado

"A deeply personal testament to the power of perseverance, the will to live, and the quest for self discovery and purpose. David's journey into higher awareness and universal truth is told with incredible love, insight and eloquence of spirit. It is a delightful delving into our shared humanity and is a magical read from cover to cover."

Robert Powell - Denver, Colorado

David has written a book that bares his soul. Footsteps After The Fall is unique and special yet available to all on similar path. We all hunger and long for those moments when the Universe speaks from within and bursts forth with new and old Truth. A universal Truth simple yet so profound. We are One and Love is the glue.

I find in this story a common occurrence for those seeking enlightenment. For David, a rock on the head. For others a lifetime sitting in a cave meditating. For myself and others our unique path.

I encourage anyone drawn to David's book to find their own story within the pages of Footsteps after the Fall. Many will realize their soul is opening out a way for this splendor to escape. To be made available to all.

David Fitzpatrick - Tucson, Arizona

"Inspiring and beautifully written. I love that you have pulled from many different realms of human experience spiritual, psychological, physiological to explain not only your experience but your theory on living rich and fulfilling lives as individuals and as caretakers of the earth and all of its creatures.

Most of all, I think you open the door for all of your readers to begin to explore the idea that life is about joy and lightness rather than darkness and suffering. You give the permission that we are all longing for to pursue our dreams and lives marked by happiness and joy rather than the sacrifice and suffering our culture and its institutions have convinced us is normal and expected.

The goings on in the world today are getting darker and heavier moment by moment. We are inundated with messages of fear and negativity. Your book and teachings are so timely and so needed at this point in history. We desperately need courageous, articulate, wise teachers like you to encourage a new way of living and being in the world."

Mindy Tomlinson - Telluride, Colorado

A must read for anyone wanting to make significant, lasting changes in their life. Through David's vivid imagery, and emotionally engaging writing style, he has taken his near death experience and turned it into a refreshing, well written guide for better understanding the energetic principles that affect our lives. Embracing these principles and learning to live by them on a daily basis opens up a world of infinite possibilities for creating meaningful, lasting changes. Having read the book and different chapters multiple times, I have come to appreciate it as a valuable resource that will be with me forever.

Micah James Page - Boulder, Colorado

ABOUT THE AUTHOR

David was interviewed by Bob Guiney, Oprah's "man on the street" and the Bachelor, as a guest on the "Success Today" TV show, which will air on NBC, ABC, CBS and FOX affiliates across the nation.

David Strauss is an internationally recognized author, speaker, coach and a human potential thought leader. David has over 20 years of experience inspiring people to improve their lives and to live with a deeper sense of purpose and meaning. His contagious smile and energy is rooted in his deep love for people, life, health, and fitness. From deep sea scuba diving to climbing to the 23,000 foot summit of one of the tallest mountains in the world, David embraces life and challenges himself and others to learn and grow.

Through his journey of healing from being hit in the head by a falling rock several years ago, David discovered his true sense of purpose. Since that time he has connected with a singular vision of wanting to have a lasting and meaningful impact on people's lives by changing how they perceive themselves and giving them the tools to become happy, healthy, focused individuals.

Recognizing the value of learning from experience, David's vision of wanting to capture the deep hidden meaning of his experience first started becoming a reality through the release of his first book, *Footsteps After The Fall*, and through the development of the Giggle Yoga Philosophy. His new book, *Dancing With Vampires*, teaches people how to take responsibility for their lives and rid themselves of negative thoughts and beliefs.

David's passion for changing peoples' lives was first nurtured at University of Colorado at Boulder where he studied Interpersonal and Small Group Communication. He has continually expanded his knowledge base through countless books and seminars. Through his studies, David has become an expert in understanding human needs psychology. This knowledge has given him powerful tools for understanding the driving force behind human behavior and has allowed him to incorporate cutting edge strategies to motivate others to lead extraordinary lives.

Through his commitment to being a global thought leader, David became a graduate of Tony Robbins Mastery University and a Joe Williams certified and endorsed professional speaker. As a result of his experience as a 2nd Lieutenant in the US Air Force Auxiliary (CAP), David became a program facilitator for the National Character and Leadership Symposium (NCLS) at the United States Air Force Academy.

As an outgrowth of his desire to help others improve their lives, David has participated in a wide variety of fundraising events for local and national charities. As a benefit for the University of Colorado Cancer Research Foundation, David and his international climbing team reached the 23,000 foot summit of Aconcagua, Argentina, the tallest mountain in the western and southern hemispheres. He has also climbed over a dozen peaks with summits greater than 14,000 feet.

Now, David sees a global opportunity to leverage the story of his personal story by creating teaching and learning tools which help people throughout the world to self-realize their own potential and to improve the quality of their lives.

David has started the Giggle Yoga Project and is continually looking for ways to create strategic relationships with other people, businesses, and thought leaders who are dedicated to improving the overall direction and welfare of humanity.

My Deepest...

Love, Thoughts and Prayers

for my Niece,

Chelsea Jacqueline China Strauss,

whose life was prematurely taken

on April 8, 2010

She was loved by all who knew her.

October 5, 1985 – April 8, 2010

CPSIA information can be obtained
at www.ICGtesting.com
Printed in the USA
FSOW04n1138131015
12118FS

9 780996 783606